Choosing the Right Thing to Do

Before   <u>Nov. 10</u>

Shapiro

- Chapter 1, 6, 7

Read
Ch 7

Saturday — Nov 10

Choosing the
Right
Thing
to Do

In Life, at Work,
in Relationships, and for
the Planet

DAVID A. SHAPIRO

Berrett-Koehler Publishers
San Francisco

Berrett-Koehler Publishers, Inc.
450 Sansome Street, Suite 1200
San Francisco, CA 94111-3320
Tel: 415-288-0260   Fax: 415-362-2512
Website: www.bkconnection.com

Ordering Information

Individual sales. Berrett-Koehler publications are available through most bookstores. They can also be ordered direct from Berrett-Koehler Publishers by calling, toll-free; 800-929-2929; fax 802-864-7626.

Quantity sales. Special discounts are available on quantity purchases by corporations, associations, and others. For details, contact the "Special Sales Department" at the Berrett-Koehler address above.

Orders for college textbook/course adoption use. Please contact Berrett-Koehler Publishers toll-free; 800-929-2929; fax 802-864-7626.

Orders by U.S. trade bookstores and wholesalers. Please contact Publishers Group West, 1700 Fourth Street, Berkeley, CA 94710; 510-528-1444; 1-800-788-3123; fax 510-528-9555.

Printed in the United States of America

 Printed on acid-free and recycled paper that is composed of 50 percent recovered fiber, including 10 percent postconsumer waste.

Library of Congress Cataloging-in-Publication Data
Shapiro, David A., 1957–
    Choosing the right thing to do / by David A. Shapiro. — 1st ed.
    p. cm.
Includes bibliographical references and index.
ISBN 1-57675-057-4 (alk. paper)
    1. Right and wrong.   2. Decision making—moral and ethical aspects.   I. Title.
BJ1411.S43 1999
170'.44—dc21   99–34077
                                                CIP

First Edition

02 01 00 99   10 9 8 7 6 5 4 3 2 1

Designed by Detta Penna

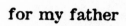

for my father

Contents

Acknowledgments

The right thing to do in a book like this is to acknowledge everyone I have ever met, for with every interaction I've learned something more about the right—and often the wrong—thing to do. So to all the people with whom I've ever crossed paths, I say thank you very much, you've taught me a lot.

That said, there are a number of people I'd like to single out, people without whose support this book would never have happened.

First, I would like to express my heartfelt gratitude to Valerie Barth, Senior Editor at Berrett-Koehler Publishers. Valerie's unwavering support for *Choosing the Right Thing to Do,* even in light of my own occasional doubts, sustained this project from start to finish. The book you are reading would not exist without her.

Second, I would like to thank the thoughtful and compassionate reviewers who read earlier drafts of *Choosing the Right Thing to Do* and gave me insightful and illuminating commentary. Burton Frierson, Kendra Armer, Alis Valencia, Mark Mendenhall, Paul Wright, and Cathie Leavitt were all much kinder and gentler with the manuscript than those early drafts warranted. Their comments provided structural as well as philosophical direction and helped make the final version infinitely stronger than the original. Anything of value that emerges from this text can be directly attributed to their assistance; all the mistakes in here are my own.

My colleagues in the doctoral program in Philosophy at the University of Washington offer me ongoing intellectual support and counsel. I would especially like to thank my dissertation chair, Dr. Jean Roberts, for allowing me the time and space to pursue this rather personal and somewhat nonacademic project.

I am indebted to Jana Mohr Lone, the director of the *Northwest Center for Philosophy for Children,* for introducing me to Philosophy for Children. Working with grade school and middle school kids in the exploration of philosophical questions is both humbling and invigorating and had much to do with how I approached writing this book.

I gladly owe Dick Leider my deepest thanks for many reasons. His generosity in allowing me to work with him in co-authoring *Repacking Your Bags* provided numerous tangible and intangible supports that led directly to this book. His helpful comments on earlier drafts of *Choosing the Right Thing to Do* helped clear up confusion in the text and my head. And his ongoing influence on my life and career as a mentor cannot be overstated.

I would like to thank all the people who appear in stories in this book. By sharing your lives, you have made *Choosing the Right Thing to Do* come alive in the world and on the page.

My wife, Jennifer Dixon, and my daughter, Amelia Grace Dixon-Shapiro, have my undying gratitude for reasons too numerous to mention. Suffice it to say that their indulgence, tolerance, and love are the primary sustenance of my life.

Finally, I would like to thank my parents who got me interested in questions of right and wrong in the first place. I am grateful to my mother for being a model of how one should speak and write about such issues. And I owe my father—who, tragically, passed away during the writing of *Choosing the Right Thing to Do*—the deepest possible debt of gratitude imaginable. His kindness, compassion, generosity, and strength of character have left a legacy of moral wisdom we all may aspire to.

A Gas Station Burns in the Forest

Illuminating our Moral Legacy

Every day, all day long, we are presented with choices: simple ones, like "Should I hit the snooze button on my alarm one more time?"; more complex ones, like "How ought I to respond when someone I care for fails to live up to my expectations?" And every day, all day long, we make these choices. We do the best we can with the information and experience we have, and we try to make choices that reflect our deepest values and are consistent with the sort of person we would like to be.

Every choice we make goes into creating who we are. With every move we make—every action, every inaction, every thought that flashes through our minds—more sand trickles from the top of life's hourglass into the bottom. Each grain of sand—every single instant we're alive—builds up to form an afterimage of who we were, where we came from, what we did, and how we loved. This

1

afterimage is our legacy, our gift to the future, the story of our life to be told after we've gone.

How will you be remembered?

When your children, grandchildren, great-grandchildren, and beyond talk about you, what will they say? Who is the person they will see when they examine the afterimage you have left behind?

Think of your own recollections of those who have preceded you: family members, friends, co-workers and colleagues, public figures great and small, the well- and the little-known. What remains of them when they are no longer here?

Possessions are disbursed, projects taken over, vital statistics catalogued away until all that's left of who we were is *who we were.*

Our character.

Our character is our legacy. And our legacy is ultimately a moral legacy. It is the story of the good and bad things we did to and for other people.

Our bequest to tomorrow will not primarily be monetary or physical or even spiritual; that is, it won't be something beyond this earthly plane. What we will grant to others in our absence is what we have granted to them in our presence: how we have met our obligations to them as family members, lovers, neighbors, colleagues, and fellow human beings.

As we proceed through life, this can be hard to see. The day-to-day responsibilities of making a living, raising a family, keeping up with the Joneses—not to mention rooting for one's favorite sports team, downloading the latest Internet software, and keeping tabs on the extramarital dalliances of world leaders—incline us to perceive ourselves as individual, autonomous agents whose legacy is more about what we *produced* than *how we lived.* While few people *really* believe that whoever dies with the most toys wins, many of us do live our lives as if our acquisitions will have a more lasting effect than our offerings.

But when we look back upon things, it becomes obvious how much more enduring is what we give than what we take. And we can see better how our legacy—both individually and as a society—is most clearly forged by the moral choices we have made.

It doesn't take a wise old person to recognize this; even a child (even a teenager!) can recognize how enduring our moral legacy really is—and how unforgettable are the choices that lead to its creation.

Here's how I know.

When I was 13, my father, my best friend, and I toured the western United States in a Winnebago motor home. During the three weeks we spent together, I enjoyed all the father and son bonding experiences a kid could hope for. I got to drive our truck on the highway. I drank my first beer straight from the can. I learned that my old man, despite his age, education, and the respect that, as a medical doctor, the world accorded him, was an imperfect human being—just like me.

Yet what I remember most about our journey is a single experience, one that lasted no more than ten minutes but which has stuck with me for some three decades now. I have often wondered why the event implanted itself so deeply in my consciousness, and it is only by considering it in light of a moral legacy that I believe I have found my answer. The event, though short-lived and personal, has come to bear a significance that is both enduring and universal; in short, it has come to represent for me the moral legacy of our time.

The picture of what happened has yellowed with age, but if I focus my mind's eye on the images, they return with the clarity of the mountain air which was their alembic.

About 300 yards outside the entrance to Glacier National Park in Montana are two gas stations, one on either side of the two-lane road. They have been strategically placed so tourists can fill up before entering the park and refill upon leaving. The one on the left is a national brand, the one on the right, a local Mom 'n Pop cut-price mark called Y-Pay-Mor. We, of course, have chosen the national brand—quality, my dad likes to reminds me, is worth a few pennies extra. Besides, the cut-rate places don't take credit cards, and gasoline, for convenience and accounting, is always purchased by credit card—that's just how it's done.

We have completed filling our vehicle's huge 32-gallon tank, have stocked up on peanuts and gum, and paid. With my father behind the wheel, me in the passenger seat, and my best friend lounging at the motor home's kitchen table, we are just beginning to pull out. It is almost dusk and we are in a hurry to find our reserved campsite before it gets dark.

Just as my father angles the Winnebago onto the road, an explosion rocks the gas station across the street. Through the corner of my window, I see a fireball engulf its white clapboard office. I perceive the image of a man inside completely on fire, staggering toward what had been the door, and rolling on the ground, over and over. A woman comes running from the back, pointing at the right side of the building where the restrooms are. She waves her arms at the blazing structure and cries "My baby! My baby is in there!"

By this time, we are on the road and pulling away. I look at my dad. "Did you see that?! Should we stop?"

He is fighting to disbelieve what he only half-saw. The expression on his face is one I've never seen before. His eyes are wide; they look simultaneously young and ancient, somehow. His jaw is clenched and his hands are tight around the steering wheel. He is slightly hunched over, as if urging our vehicle forward. He focuses on the road ahead, hits the brakes as a man in jeans and a T-shirt sprints across in front of us and toward the fire, then accelerates again.

"Dad! There was a guy, I think, on fire! Shouldn't we do something?"

My dad says that he didn't see any guy and even if there was, there's nothing we can do. It's too dangerous and there are other people already on the scene. It's better we should hurry up to the park entrance and tell the rangers.

When we get there, a small crowd has assembled and is looking back at the plume of black smoke that is now funneling upwards. One park ranger is inside the toll booth, talking hurriedly on the phone. A second stands outside with his arms folded, watching the smoke rise, looking bewildered. My father explains to him what has happened. The ranger gratefully acknowledges the information, tells us it will help, and says that we should move inside the park so emergency vehicles can get through.

We drive off toward our campground. I ask my father if we should go back after we get set up.

"We've done the best we could do," he says. "The right people have been informed. It's under control now."

That's the last we ever talk about it.

Did we do the right thing? What is the moral legacy of the choice we made? How does it mirror the moral legacy of our time? As I recall what happened and as I consider how our society will be remembered, I see many similarities between this microcosmic memory and the macrocosmic legacy we as a people will leave behind.

I begin by considering the setting, which strikes me as a particularly apt metaphor for this day and age—two gas stations outside a National Park. Note that one of the stations is a corporate franchise; it's a clean, well-lighted place. The other, unsupported by the conglomerate, is a dilapidated shanty. The former serves well-to-do customers, people who tour National Parks in Winnebagos, who pay by credit card, who think that a tidy bathroom and monthly statements of account are worth the extra cost. Customers at the latter pay by cash, they drive beat-up station wagons and camp outside, in tents or under the stars. To them, gas is gas—why pay more?

Tragedy strikes. Tragically, it strikes the less affluent station. Hasn't this been the trend throughout the 20th century, particularly when technology is involved? Bhopal, Chernobyl, the Marshall Islands—time and time again, less-developed places bear the brunt of the technology that sustains more developed ones.

Why did *Y-Pay-Mor* and not our station explode? Were its owners cutting corners on safety in order to keep up with their corporate-supported competitor across the street? Or were they simply not as well-informed as to the dangers? Perhaps they didn't have the resources—educational or financial—to guarantee a sufficient degree of safety. Or maybe they were just unlucky. Again, it appears to be a peculiar feature of our shared moral legacy that bad things seem to happen to underprivileged people, whether through negligence, conspiracy, or just plain bad luck.

Next, I see us driving away—in a motor home, no less—as a man burns and a mother screams for her child. Conceivably, we could have stopped and done something, but we didn't. I consider all the reasons that modern society doesn't stop and do something and the explanations seem identical.

First, we are afraid. Afraid for ourselves, of course, but even more, we are afraid for our loved ones, and most of all, for our children.

My father has his son next to him; his son's best friend—the child of his own dear friend, a youngster he has known since the boy was born—sits nearby, and across the street, not 50 yards away, a gas station office has exploded. He doesn't know why, or what might happen next. My father is a physician, not an engineer. Who knows where the underground tanks of petroleum are located? Who knows if the whole station might suddenly ignite? Maybe both stations share some sort of underground storage—the entire road could blow. At the very least, we are carrying 32 gallons of gasoline ourselves. We've got to get away, and get away quickly. We must remove ourselves and our families from any potential danger.

One doesn't have to sift carefully through the legacy of our time to see how fear has colored our moral choices. Our silent response to atrocities, from the turn of the century to the dawning of the new millennium, bears mute testimonial to our lack of the moral virtue known as courage.

Of course, we also don't know how we can help—if at all. We're too late, we don't have the skills, nothing can be done. My father says that if the man really were on fire, no one could save him. We don't do anything because we think what we could won't be enough. What difference will it make anyway?

As a society, we take this same moral stance. Our legacy is one of inaction—not simply through lack of compassion, but through lack of knowledge. We're paralyzed because we feel powerless. We're silent because we feel dumb. If no one can do anything, why should we?

Besides, we do what we can. We report the accident to the proper agency. We let those in charge take care of things. After all, that's what they're there for. We get out of the way so they can do their jobs. Those people are experts; they know what they're doing. If anyone's in trouble, they'll see to it that people are cared for.

Isn't this the code of behavior that most of us have accepted? We assume that the experts will solve our problems for us. We don't lose sleep—not too much, anyway—over the hole in the ozone, or the destruction of the rain forest, or how to dispose of nuclear waste, because we know that somewhere, somebody is making everything all right. We just have to let them know what's happening, and they'll figure it out. As a result, we can look back and know that—despite our inaction—we did our part, small as it was. But our descendants—if there are any—what will they think? Will they look at our failure to take personal action and assume that we didn't care?

But we do care. We just have to get on with our lives. It's getting dark. We still have many miles to go. We've never been here before. We're tired and hungry. How can we help anyone when we're in this state of mind? We've got to get our own act together before we can help others, don't we?

I know that many people nowadays—myself included—often feel this way. I recognize this attitude as a healthy component of our survival instinct and one that enables us to carry on so we can make additional choices—moral or not—that sustain us. But I wonder what our world would be like if this survival-first message was the moral legacy of Socrates or of Martin Luther King, Jr., or of Gandhi.

Another reason we don't act is because we don't trust our senses. The information that comes in gets filtered and hazy. Our brains raise a gauzy protective shield. Ultimately, we get to the point where we wonder what really did happen. Did we actually see what we thought we saw? History recedes, disappearing into a murkier and murkier past. Ironically, one of our most significant contributions to posterity, personally and as a society, is amnesia.

I remember thinking back on the explosion less than an hour afterward and asking myself if it really happened. We couldn't see the flames or the black plume of smoke anymore; there was no sign of the explosion or smell of burning gasoline on our bodies—what if I just imagined the whole thing? The woman crying for her baby—wasn't that a scene from a TV show? The image of the man on fire—wasn't that a photo in *Life*?

If anything best defines the moral legacy of our time, it's forgetfulness. We can overlook anything: World War I, the Holocaust, the Atomic Bomb. Sooner or later, our memories of such horrors fade; the parts we have played in them slip from our recollections.

But, of course, these are the very things we *most* need to remember, for they are the very things we will most be remembered for: they are our legacy.

So now, when I think back at what happened that day in Montana and how we reacted, I believe that we did not do the right thing. It seems wrong to me that we didn't at least stop. It seems wrong because my father *did* have special skills. He was a physician and perhaps his expertise would have been useful—especially in such a remote area.

I wish we had taken the time—and had the ability—to more carefully consider what we ought to have done. I believe now, in retrospect, we would have behaved quite differently.

What we did seems wrong to me because we didn't make an effort to find out more. We didn't take our time. We let our fear rule us. Instead of moving on to safety and then looking back to learn how we could help, we pushed forward, to even higher ground. We washed our hands of the affair rather than risk dirtying them by at least trying to discover what we could do.

Finally, and perhaps most important, the moral legacy of this incident—and, by extension, of our time—seems a poor one because afterward, we never talked about it. We never discussed our behavior and examined what we might have done differently. We never considered together how we might behave next time. We permitted our shame and embarrassment over our inaction—which perhaps we sensed instinctively was wrong—to inhibit us from sharing our thoughts and feelings. As a result, we never made the effort to learn from our mistakes. This, I feel, is the sorriest aspect of our legacy of all.

Our legacy—personal and societal—is a product of what we leave behind after we are gone. Three events go into its creation: the incidents that occurred, how we acted during them, and how we reacted afterward. Recalling a singular, personal incident, I reflect on our collective moral legacy. No one can deny that terrible things have happened. Nevertheless, no one has to accept total responsibility for their occurrence. No one should bear that burden.

What we can take responsibility for—and what we must—is how we act *now*. Our moral legacy is still being formed, and it is still possible to craft it well. For it's not by our actions during events, but rather by our reaction afterward that, ultimately, we confirm our moral legacy. This is our gift to tomorrow and how our descendants shall memorialize or revile us.

Our Moral Legacy

Our own moral legacy is the heritage of attitudes we have and actions we take on issues of right and wrong. It is the tapestry we weave in and through these attitudes and actions. Our moral legacy is the living document we write for others to read our character from. It is both a reflection of and a statement about who we are, one that travels with us throughout our life and carries on after we pass away.

Examining the questions we face in light of our moral legacy can therefore help us behave in ways that more accurately reflect our deepest, most abiding values. When we recognize how our choices create our moral legacy, we will want to make sure those choices are indeed the best we can make. At the very least, taking into account our moral legacy may inspire us to critically evaluate our choices so as to improve upon them. What we see in the mirror may not always be what we want to see, but seeing it clearly is the first step toward changing what needs to be changed.

What is your moral legacy?

And, just as important, is the legacy you're creating an accurate reflection of who you really are? Are people able to see what you truly cherish by examining the choices you have made?

It is the most important question we ever ask ourselves: "What ought I to do?" And it's even more important in light of our moral legacy.

We won't end up looking back on our lives regretting or celebrating the choices we made about toothpaste brand or athletic shoe model. We will review things and say, "I shoulda, oughtta, coulda..." about the *big* questions:

How ought I to treat my loved ones? What does it mean to be a good parent? How can I tell if I'm behaving fairly toward my co-workers and clients?

On our deathbeds, we won't wonder about our careers or our possessions or our wardrobes. Rather, we will ask ourselves:

Did I live a good life? Did I do the right thing? Was I a person my children and grandchildren can respect?

So it's quite odd, given the importance of these questions, that we typically get so little help in answering them. And why, individually and collectively, we often do such a sorry job of choosing the right thing to do.

But it isn't hopeless. Each of us is born with the potential for making excellent choices. We all have the basic sensibilities necessary for properly assessing what we ought to do and for choosing appropriately. It's just a matter of refining these sensibilities and improving our willingness to act on the proper choices we make.

That's what *Choosing the Right Thing to Do* is all about.

The central thesis of this book is that each of us can learn to make better choices—choices that more accurately reflect our deepest values and that, as a result, are more likely to sustain and enhance the moral legacy we hope to leave. This, of course, assumes there *are* better and worse choices, and *Choosing the Right Thing to Do* investigates that question as well.

The process by which we learn to better perceive and choose the right thing to do is quite natural. It involves learning to hold in our minds—and our hearts—the particular issue at hand in order to examine it from as many perspectives as possible. This examination, which seeks to consider a full spectrum of appropriate responses, enables us to come to a deeper, richer, and more complete expression of our values. And, in doing so, it allows us to make better, more sophisticated judgments about what we ought to do.

Behind *Choosing the Right Thing to Do* is the idea of practical wisdom explored by the ancient Greek philosopher Aristotle in his classic *Nichomachean Ethics*. Broadly, practical wisdom—*phronesis*—is the intellectual component of virtue. It is knowledge of how to secure the good life, which for Aristotle is happiness. Practical wisdom involves the ability to consider the range of choices that one faces in any situation and the willingness to choose whatever action coordinates with one's properly chosen goals. Above all, Aristotle concludes, practical wisdom must be a "reasoned and true capacity to act with regard to human goods."[1] Having practical wisdom, therefore, enables us to achieve these goods; ultimately, being practically wise enables us to attain true happiness: the good life.

In my previous book, *Repacking Your Bags: Lighten Your Load for the Rest of Your Life*, which I co-wrote with life- and career-planning expert Dick Leider, we explored a contemporary notion of the good

---

[1]Aristotle, *Nichomachean Ethics*, Book VI, Chapter 5.

life, which was defined as *"living in the place you belong, with the people you love, doing the right work, on purpose." Choosing the Right Thing to Do* continues that exploration, examining our moral legacy in light of these four components of the good life: place, love, work, and purpose. It is intended to help readers make better choices at work, in personal relationships, for the planet, and on purpose.

The Moral Spectrum

Throughout *Choosing the Right Thing to Do,* I use the metaphor of a moral spectrum to reinforce the idea that the important issues we deal with in our lives rarely have black or white answers. Nor does it really capture their complexity to say they're gray. Rather, they are typically multicolored and many-hued. Every day, we encounter innumerable shades of right and wrong; we have to discriminate among them to choose wisely. And our moral responses, like the colors of the spectrum, are dependent not only on what we observe, but also on how we observe them. The notion of the moral spectrum thus serves to remind us that unless our own faculties of perception are kept in tune, moral blindness is an ever-present possibility.

In keeping with that theme, *Choosing the Right Thing to Do,* like the visible spectrum, is organized into seven distinct sections whose edges, nevertheless, blend smoothly into one another.

Chapter 1, "The Color of Moral: What Makes Right Acts Right?" investigates the very nature of rightness and wrongness. What makes right acts right and wrong acts wrong? People have long wondered what moral properties are, whether they exist independently of our judgments or whether they are merely expressions of people's attitudes. In this chapter, I try to mediate this dispute, proposing instead that a reasonable analogy can be made between moral properties and properties like color—which, though they do depend on our input to be perceived, still have an objectivity independent of what individually we think of them.

Chapter 2, "The Moral Spectrum: Broadening Our Perspective on the Right Thing To Do," examines a methodology for improving our perception of rightness and wrongness. This process has the virtue of enriching our ability to make finer moral discriminations and, in doing so, to presumably make better choices. Like a painter who, through practice, learns to see colors that once were indiscriminate to her, each of us can come to a richer appreciation of the many shades of moral judgment and thus make more informed, more sophisticated choices.

Chapter 3, "Right at Work: Doing Right by Co-workers and Customers," looks at the ways in which businesspeople and the organizations for which they work can refine their moral sensibilities. What qualifies as an appropriate moral stance for a business to take? Does profit justify choices that we would otherwise see as morally objectionable? How do we reconcile our obligations to members of the diverse communities whom, as businesspeople, we serve? These and other such questions are addressed here, drawing upon interviews, conversations, and conferences with contemporary businesspeople and consultants.

Chapter 4, "Right in Love: Doing Right by Friends, Family Members, and Loved Ones," explores the question "How ought I to behave toward my loved ones?" What is the right thing to do in interactions with friends and family members? How can I be a good partner, parent, confidante? It offers a simple, well-known, but sometimes misunderstood principle for helping us to sustain long-lasting, meaningful, and mutually rewarding relationships.

Chapter 5, "Right in Place: Doing Right by the Planet," examines the relationship between our environment and the right thing to do. We can learn much about the quality of our choices by examining our connection to the natural world. Poets, philosophers, naturalists—thoughtful people of all stripes—consistently admonish us to draw upon the lessons of nature in determining what we ought to do in our transactions with each other. In this chapter, we follow in the footsteps of thinkers like Thoreau, Emerson, and Wendell Berry to clear a pathway toward improved moral judgment.

Chapter 6, "Right on Purpose: Doing Right by Yourself," offers advice for making the ability to perceive and choose the right thing to do an integral component of one's character. It looks at how we often think we'll be happier by doing what we know we shouldn't—and only later discover that we were wrong. In response, it provides some suggestions for how to embrace the right thing to do and, in doing so, discover the higher pleasures of virtue.

Finally, *Chapter 7,* "Doing the Best We Can Do: Reflections on Our Moral Legacy," reexamines how we can continually improve our choice making, in hopes of creating a moral legacy that reflects upon us in the best light possible. Chapter 7 offers a way to re-evaluate our choices in light of the "big picture." This is meant to keep us on track with our most deeply felt moral intuitions and in touch with the moral sensibilities that guide the progress of our lives.

Morality Without Moralizing

Not all the "ought" questions we face in our lives are moral ones. There are also pragmatic or practical concerns: Ought I to brush my teeth or not?; legal questions: Would it be all right for me to jaywalk here?; matters of etiquette: How wrong would it be to use the large fork on my salad?

But certainly, the "oughts" associated with moral issues are the most important we have to deal with. They are the most telling reflections of our characters—both who we are and who we aspire to be. They are the choices that create the legacy we will leave behind—individually, and as a society.

Consequently, assistance in choosing the morally right thing to do is sought by all quarters. Parents and educators are hungry for solutions to help them instill a sense of moral responsibility in young people. Businesspeople, pulled in conflicting directions by conscience and competition, reach out longingly for moral guidance. Concerned citizens struggle—both alone and in groups—with emerging moral dilemmas occasioned by new technologies, societal changes, and other upheavals in their individual and collective lives.

Choosing the Right Thing to Do is intended to provide some help in coming to grips with these and other quite troubling moral issues. In doing so, it stresses the rich heritage of pluralism at the core of our shared experience. *Choosing the Right Thing to Do* does not take any one particular political stand; it does, however, draw upon our long-standing liberal tradition, which stresses free trade in the marketplace of ideas, allowing the truth to be forged in the crucible of informed discussion.

Moreover, in *Choosing the Right Thing to Do,* I offer no theological view, although my approach is informed by a perspective that tries not to separate the spiritual from the worldly. Nor do I argue for a single ethical principle, like many of philosophy's great thinkers. On the contrary; *Choosing the Right Thing to Do* attempts to weave together diverse strands of thought on moral issues to form a tapestry that blankets a variety of conflicting viewpoints.

It should be noted that in *Choosing the Right Thing to Do,* I am not moralizing. I am not trying to tell other people what they ought or ought not to do. That task I leave to parents, teachers, religious leaders, and afternoon talk-show hosts. Instead, *Choosing the Right Thing to Do* introduces a number of principles to help people determine the right thing to do *for themselves.* This does not, however, imply that "anything goes." Rather, one of the main messages of *Choosing the Right Thing to Do* is that right and wrong do matter; there are indeed better and worse choices to be made. Nevertheless, the best choices are usually made by the people most directly affected by them.

Consequently, *Choosing the Right Thing to Do* is unabashedly pragmatic. Theory takes a backseat to application. Professional philosophers reading this book will no doubt have justifiable complaints about some of the theoretical interpretations I have made. My hope, however, is that the practical value of what readers can take away from *Choosing the Right Thing to Do* may excuse some scholarly liberty. If I have sacrificed rigor for accessibility, so be it. It seems to me that the importance of having a rich array of perspectives for determining the right thing to do warrants some flexibility in their presentation.

The 20th-century American philosopher and educator John Dewey wrote: "Moral theory cannot emerge when there is a positive belief as to what is right and what is wrong, for then there is no occasion for reflection. It emerges when men are confronted with situations in which different desires promise opposed goods and in which incompatible courses of action seem to be morally justified. Only such a conflict calls forth personal inquiry into the bases of morals."[2]

The complexity of modern society and the consequent moral questions each of us face represents the perfect environment for moral theory to emerge. Every one of us regularly confronts situations in which the right thing to do isn't exactly clear. It's often hard to tell how we should behave toward our friends and loved ones, co-workers and colleagues, neighbors and fellow citizens. Different duties—to our families, our jobs, our communities—pull us in different directions. Opposing desires—for success, for free time, for social intercourse—make it difficult for us to determine what's right and what's wrong. We need, therefore, to think carefully about why we feel we should act one way and not another. We need, as Dewey says, to find our way out of moral perplexity through reflection upon the enduring principles that underlie our most deeply held moral values.

Let us then begin that personal inquiry by considering the basis of morality itself in Chapter 1, "The Color of Moral: What Makes Right Acts Right?"

---

[2]Dewey, John, *Theory of the Moral Life*, (NY: Henry Holt, 1932), p. 17.

The Color of Moral

What Makes Right Acts Right?

What Makes Good Things Good and Bad Things Bad?

Do you cheat on your taxes? On your spouse? Do you steal money from your friends? Do you regularly make solemn promises to your kids that you have no intention of keeping?

Probably not. But why not? Is it simply that you're afraid of getting caught? Or is there something more? Don't you also have a feeling that cheating, stealing, and lying are wrong?

Probably so. But why? What is it about cheating, stealing, and lying that makes them wrong? For that matter, what is it about fairness, generosity, and honesty that makes them right? How come there's such a difference between the things we feel we should do and the things we feel we shouldn't?

It's a question I've wondered about for a long, long time:

What, in other words, makes the good things good and the bad things bad?

It's 1970, and I'm in seventh grade at Fulton Elementary School in Pittsburgh, Pennsylvania. Monday afternoons, our class rides the bus across town to manual-arts magnet classes. It is a noble experiment on the part of our local educational administrators for a couple of reasons. First, because it brings together kids from our relatively well-to-do neighborhood with students from neighborhoods that aren't so economically advantaged. And second, because it is the first time that all students, boys and girls alike, take the full range of manual-arts offerings. This means that on any given Monday, I'm just as likely to be burning bran muffins in home economics class as my friend, Debbie Fiedler, is to be bending nails in wood shop.

For our part, though, it's a drag on any number of counts. First, because it means that the bigger and tougher kids from the other schools get to spend their Monday afternoons torturing us from the moment we pick them up after lunch to the second our shared bus drops them off after school. And second, because the bus ride adds at least an hour to our school day, which means that not only is the usual agony worse than normal, it's longer, too.

So, often we conspire to alleviate the pain by treating ourselves to something special when we get back home: maybe a movie, or a Pirates game if it's baseball season, or just a session of pinball at the local deli—anything to adjust our prepubescent attitudes in light of the traumatic experience we've just been through. (The following year, we realize we can achieve the same effect by skipping manual-arts class altogether, but at this point, in seventh grade, we aren't so creative.)

On this particular Monday, my three best friends—Paul, Michael, Willie—and I have arranged to go to see a Charlie Chaplin revival that is playing a couple miles from where we all live. Michael's mom has agreed to leave work early and drive us, but only on the condition that we promise to show up promptly. The movie is at 4:15, so, since the bus usually drops us off at 4:00, we are cutting it pretty close. But with the optimism about schedules that tends to afflict preteenagers, we're confident we can make it.

The day is memorable in part because I have been making a shirt in sewing class and, since I don't believe that the pattern we are working from could possibly be right, have ended up cutting off the material for both sleeves and the collar yoke, effectively turning the shirt into a fringed vest, complete with fraying armholes and raveling bottom seams. Still, I'm excited to show off my creation and proudly sport it over my polo shirt on the bus ride home. This causes William Goosby, one of my usual Monday afternoon tormentors, to amp up his customary level of tormenting, augmenting the standard body-pokes with loud aspersions about my sexual orientation and, even worse, comparisons between my outfit and one he's seen David Cassidy wearing on "The Partridge Family Show." Understandably, I am even more eager than usual to get home and off the bus as quickly as possible.

So, when we're pulling up to school and the bus driver eases slowly over to the curb, I can hardly stand it. When he takes his time turning off the bus, I'm about to burst. And when he fails to immediately open the door to let us exit, I can't take it any more.

I suggest to my friends that we leave by the windows. Willie is hesitant, but I argue that if we move quickly, the bus driver won't even know we've left, so what difference does it make? We'll be happier and no one else will suffer at all. Michael is skeptical, so I tell him to think about his mom; we've promised her we'll be on time and we're already late. Don't we owe her doing whatever it takes to get there as fast as possible? Paul is unsure but I claim that since we aren't the kind of kids who do bad things and get in trouble, what is the problem? As long as it's us, and not say, William Goosby climbing out, how can it be wrong?

As we're lowering the windows, Amy Schubert tells us to stop; we're supposed to leave by the front door; that's what the rules say. I say she ought to trust her feelings more; it doesn't feel wrong, so how could there possibly be anything wrong with what we're doing?

By this time, my three friends are already sliding down the outside of the bus and sprinting away. I give up trying to persuade Amy to see things my way and squeeze my head through the metal-framed panes.

As I begin lowering myself to the ground outside, I feel a strong pair of hands grasp me about the waist and pull me violently to the ground.

"What the hell do you think you're doing!"

The bus driver digs his fingers into my shoulders and immobilizes me against the bus. "Are you trying to get me fired? Or just break your neck? We're going to see the principal about this!"

As he marches me forcibly to the office of our principal, Dr. Marshall, I sputter something about the unfairness of being singled out for punishment. "If a hundred people murdered somebody, would it be fair to punish just one of them?"

The bus driver tells me to shut up and not to worry about anyone else but myself. He knows there are plenty of others and they'll get what's coming to them, too.

In Dr. Marshall's office, she gives me the ultimatum: either I tell them who the other kids who jumped off the bus are, or our entire class will be punished.

"How is that fair?" I want to know. "And besides, what did we do that was so wrong, anyhow? Nobody got hurt and if the bus driver hadn't made such a big deal out of it, the whole thing would be done with by now."

Dr. Marshall says that she isn't here to debate with me. We have broken the rules and are to be punished, end of story.

But what rules? Where did it say you aren't allowed to leave a school bus through the windows? Nobody ever told us. The rules aren't written down.

Dr. Marshall's patience with me is already pushed beyond its breaking point. "It doesn't matter that no one ever told you. Nor that the rules are not in writing. Nor what you think about any of this. The simple fact is—and all that matters is—what you and your friends did was wrong. And that's why you're going to be punished. Because it was wrong."

"But," I cry, tears springing to my eyes as the reality of how much trouble I am in finally begins sinking in, "How do you know it's wrong? How do you know?"

Ultimately, Dr. Marshall was right: it didn't matter what I thought, or even what I did. Despite the fact that I didn't confess their involvement, Paul, Michael, and Willie got in trouble anyway. As close as we were, it was obvious to our teachers who else had to be involved if I was. But of course, this wasn't obvious to my friends, who were certain that I had squealed and shunned me for weeks—until I was the first one among us to manage to buy some beer, but that's another story. Plus, our whole class got in trouble merely by association with us and were all mad at me for weeks, too. But in spite of all that, I was still never convinced we did anything wrong.

More important, I still never got an answer to the question I asked Dr. Marshall: "How do you know it's wrong? How do you know?"

How do you know what's wrong?

The history of philosophy is littered with attempts to answer that question. In a dialogue called the *Euthyphro*, the ancient Greek philosopher Plato explored the idea that something is right or wrong depending on whether it is loved by the gods or not. This gave rise to the famous question, "Is it right because it's loved by the gods, or is it loved by the gods because it's right?" Plato leaves the answer open to interpretation, and in the absence of a definitive explanation, we are left still wondering.

Aristotle, Plato's pupil, argued that right actions are those done by the right people in the right way at the right time for the right reasons. While this does a pretty good job of indicating which actions are right and which aren't, it still doesn't tell us *why* they are.

In the 18th century, Immanuel Kant, one of Western philosophy's most important ethical theorists, claimed that rightness and wrongness are inextricably bound up in duty. By a process of reasoning alone, said Kant, we can determine what our moral duties are. Objections to this view typically revolve around questions of how something that's connected only to our thoughts and not to our emotions can possibly give us any motivation to act. The conclusions of reason are not desires, so even if we conclude that something is the right thing to do, how will this impel us to do it?

The 19th century saw the development of a theory that most of us probably take for granted as a way of choosing the right thing to do: utilitarianism. John Stuart Mill, expounding upon the views of Jeremy Bentham, proposed that actions are right insofar as they tend to promote overall happiness. As common-sensical as this sounds, it nevertheless leads to difficulties in calculating happiness, as well as to problematic situations that seem to permit individual suffering in the name of societal well-being.

Nowadays, philosophers, theologians, educators, businesspeople, and politicians continue this long-running project to provide a criterion for moral rightness. Any number of proposals are floated. What's right are the principles that rational beings would choose to govern themselves by, assuming they had no knowledge of who they were in the society in which they live. What's right is what God commands us to do. What's right is what feels right. What's right is what maximizes quality and profit without compromising our goal of being a responsible corporate citizen. What's right is anything that's not specifically prohibited by law.

The point of all this is not to give an abbreviated (and overly simplified) history of philosophy; rather, it is to illustrate how varied are the perspectives we bring to moral reasoning. And it's to suggest that often our moral dilemmas are not so much a disagreement about what is right or wrong but about what *makes something* right or wrong.

Consider the story that opened this chapter. Note the variety of perspectives on the rightness of what we were planning to do. Willie was moved by a broadly utilitarian appeal. Michael responded to what might be construed as a somewhat Kantian justification. Paul is sympathetic to a perspective that was vaguely Aristotelian. Looking back, I can take my retort to Amy as reflective of a position like that of the philosopher David Hume, which takes moral properties to be expressions of our sentiments. The bus driver was coming from a theory that based right and wrong in a sort of social contract, while Dr. Marshall seemed to be arguing from a moral theory based on authoritarian grounds.

None of this is to suggest that there isn't a way to settle the issue of whether what we did was right or wrong—in fact, I think you'd be hard-pressed to make a case that allowing 13-year-old boys to leap from the windows of school buses is in any way acceptable—rather, it is meant to illustrate that, often, what we take to be a disagreement over the rightness or wrongness of a given action isn't that at all. Instead, it's a difference in the criteria on which we're basing our judgment.

It's similar to one person saying a restaurant is lousy because the portions are small while another says it's excellent because the service is fast. They might argue about the quality of the place for hours, never realizing that at the core of their argument is a misunderstanding about what they're even arguing about. And never realizing that, as a matter of fact, they're both in serious agreement about the lousy small portions and the excellent fast service.

Of course, there are big differences between assessments of restaurant quality and judgments of morality. Not the least is that the former are merely matters of taste, while the latter are matters that go beyond mere preference. While there's no "best" favorite dining establishment, few of us want to maintain that there are no better and worse moral values to hold. And even the die-hard relativist is apt to argue for the values (tolerance, for one) that he or she holds most dear—which only goes to show that as far as our experience is concerned, we *do* treat moral values as something about which people can be mistaken and of which their judgments— through education and persuasion—can be improved.

Relatively Speaking, It's Not All Relative

All of us, at one time or another—and many of us, at *many* times or another—have made what we obviously recognize as the *wrong move*. You know, the *wrong move*: deciding to start tearing up the old linoleum on your kitchen floor at 5:30 in the afternoon on a Sunday. Or figuring you can save a few dollars by cutting your own hair the night before that big presentation for your boss. Or drinking a few beers and coming up with the idea of playing catch with bricks. The *wrong move*. A recipe for disaster. A supposedly fun thing you'll never do again.

In matters practical, financial, or work-related, we tend to easily identify one choice as better than another. The decision to take that "short-cut" on the way to the airport was a bad one. The choice not to invest in your brother-in-law's multilevel marketing scheme was good.

And yet, oddly, we tend not to be so forthright when it comes to matters of greater import: matters of moral concern. While we have no problem admitting we made even a relatively major bad financial decision—"I did a bad thing by investing heavily in last month's hot new Internet-based communications protocol," for instance—we're reticent to cop to even somewhat minor moral mistakes: "No, it wasn't wrong to insult the hotel clerk for losing my reservation; handling irate customers is part of her job and she just has to deal with it."

This isn't to say that we don't pass moral judgments on ourselves and others; five minutes listening to talk radio demonstrates beyond a shadow of a doubt that we do. Rather, the point is we're far less convinced about the reality of our moral judgments than we are of our other judgments—and given the important role that the former play in our lives, this seems strange.

Many of us, at one time or another, have been sympathetic to a moral position commonly known as "ethical relativism." Essentially, this amounts to the belief that moral judgments reflect nothing more than the opinion of the person making them. To say, for example, "slavery is wrong" means only that "I think slavery is wrong." And just because I think it is doesn't *really* mean it is. You might say, "slavery is just fine," and that's an equally valid position. Even though our views differ, they're both true; yours is just true for you, mine is true for me.

When we're asked to justify this position, we typically respond by saying something like, "Well, who are we to judge someone else? What gives us the right to say that they are doing something wrong when we're not in their shoes?"

But why do we think we don't have this right? After all, we'd have few qualms about telling someone he was wrong if he added up 2 plus 2 and got 5. Why should matters of morality be so different? Typically, we respond by saying, "Well, I just don't think I ought to *impose* my beliefs on someone else. I wouldn't want them imposing theirs on me." This, I think, reveals the heart of the matter:

It's not passing judgment we're concerned about, it's tolerance.

In our reticence to say that someone else is mistaken in their moral beliefs, we are quite rightly advocating tolerance of others' views. When we say "Just because *I* think slavery is wrong doesn't mean it is," we're implying that, in spite of the wrongness of slavery, it would be equally wrong—or worse, even—to forcibly require another culture to end its slave-holding practices. And while there might be room for debate about this (depending on how abhorrent those practices were), it's easy enough to see that this is a different judgment than the one about slavery.

When we recognize this distinction, many of us come to see that we are not nearly as relativistic in our moral beliefs as we thought we were. We recognize that having respect for other people's autonomy does not require us to admit that "anything goes." We conclude that being tolerant doesn't mean we have to be moral relativists. We can, in other words, judge someone's moral position to be wrong while simultaneously judging that it would be wrong to punch that person in nose for his beliefs.

With this realization, we recognize an inherent problem of

relativism: it contradicts itself. Suppose, as relativists, we hold that any moral view is as good as any other. Now suppose that someone else holds a view that says only his moral view is right; everyone else's is wrong. As relativists, we can't simultaneously accept this view along with our own. We are committed to the claim that everyone's view is as good any everyone else's. Even relativists, in other words, are *not* relativistic about one thing—the value of relativism.

But Isn't Everyone a Moral Expert?

Suppose we agree that right and wrong are not entirely relative. Wouldn't it still be the case that whatever people think is right for them *really is* right for them? Isn't everyone a moral expert when it comes to his or her own moral questions?

Good question!

We all may think we are—at least occasionally—but we can't be. In this way, it's a bit like matters of style. The vast majority of us think we look pretty good, but, on reflection, those in sweatpants and Birkenstocks have to yield the floor to couples in custom-cut designer outfits and handmade Italian shoes. Of course, someone might object, "Yes, but sweats and Birkies are *my* style and I feel comfortable in them!" Notice, however, that no one is disputing that.

The claim is simply that *some* people have a better sense of style than others. It should be no more contentious than claiming that some people are better at math than others. Or that we can recognize people with artistic talent versus the rest of us who can barely sign our names legibly. But if you still disagree, just go to Milan or Florence. See if you don't think the locals in their tasteful finery don't look better than tourists in plaid Bermuda shorts and black knee socks.

When it comes to ethical matters, this same story holds true. No doubt you've come across someone in your life who has a particularly well-developed moral sense. Someone who just seems to know the right thing to do. This is the person of practical wisdom, the person who could be picked up and set down in virtually any setting and still be able to make the right choices.

My dad was this sort of person. He had an uncanny knack for assessing situations and making the right move. This doesn't mean, however, that he never made mistakes; as the story in the Introduction illustrated, he sometimes failed to choose the right thing to do. Nor does it imply that he was perfectly benign and mellow. On the contrary. As Aristotle said, a necessary quality of virtuous people is that they be temperate in their emotions; that is, that they be emotional for the right reasons at the right time. Righteous anger or heartfelt sorrow certainly fit into this picture.

I'll never forget one time my father displayed the former, quite strongly—and quite rightly.

I am eight years old and want only one thing: to be Zorro, the famous swashbuckling swordsman. Make that two things: I also want a sword, so I can swashbucklingly carve "Z's" into the chests of my slain enemies as I ride away into the sunset. I beg and plead for my dad to buy me a rapier like Zorro's, but with an interest in my safety (not to mention my older sister's and the cat's) he refuses. Finally, though, after weeks of my pestering, he reluctantly agrees to make me a sword. But it would be a broadsword, made from wood, and consequently, much less likely to put out someone's eye.

My father, not a particularly handy man, struggles over his basement workbench with a hacksaw to cut my sword from a square of three-quarter inch thick plywood. Then, he carefully rounds all the edges of the cutout, the better to keep me from getting splinters and from passing them on to my sister and the cat. Having completed this time-consuming step (his only file is the three-inch hasp on his army knife), he presents the sword to me with the admonition not to stab myself with it.

I, of course, as self-centered as only an eight-year old can be, am dissatisfied with his effort and insist the sword have a black leather grip just like Zorro's. My dad, with a sigh, packs me into the car for a trip to the hardware store where we purchase a roll of black electrical tape to make the sword's handle. But even after this is completed, I want more. Zorro's sword is monogrammed; mine has to be too. My dad roots around in the attic to find his old wood-burning kit and supervises me as I burn my initials into the sword's blade. Confident that now the project is complete, he puts the kit away and prepares to head to his study for a well-deserved respite from my demands. But I stomp my foot and insist that the sword has to be shiny like Zorro's. My dad tries to convince me that the natural wood grain is more authentic but I refuse to budge. Obviously at the end of his rope, my dad locates an old can of gold paint and says that if I want my sword to be shiny, I can paint it myself.

"But," he adds in no uncertain terms, "only if you promise not to paint anything but the sword. I don't want to see any of this gold paint on the walls or the stairs or the floor."

I assure him that my brush will only touch the sword. No sooner does he leave, though, than I take his warning to be a dare and begin slapping gold paint all over the basement walls. I proudly paint "Dave is great! Signed, Zorro." in huge block letters along the basement steps.

Dad knows something is up when I come upstairs covered in paint. He disappears for a moment and then returns, quite furious, righteously angry. "You deliberately broke a promise you made. This is inexcusable."

He scoops me up, carries me to my room, and for one of the few times in my childhood gives me a spanking. The pain on my bottom doesn't last long; the memory of my broken promise never fades.

No doubt my father could have done something else less dramatic, but it wouldn't have been so memorable—or so effective. His righteous anger, coupled with his judicious use of corporal punishment, was entirely warranted. In fact, I consider what he did to be a gesture of respect. He didn't patronize me. I got the punishment I deserved and more importantly, learned the message that it intended to send. Never again did I—well, so stupidly and unthinkingly, at least—break a promise to him. As I look back, I remain convinced that he did the right thing.

So What Do Moral Experts Have That Others Don't?

How did my dad so consistently know the right thing to do? For that matter, how does anyone with a talent for making wise moral choices do so? When we see people with practical wisdom in action, it's not obvious how they do it. They make it look easy, effortless, natural.

I watched a schoolteacher friend of mine calmly defuse the anger of the father of one of his fifth-grade students. The dad was upset because his son had been prohibited from participating in the school's Christmas pageant due to inappropriate behavior on the playground. The father thought that the punishment was excessive and that, moreover, it wasn't the business of the school to discipline his child; he'd take care of that at home. When the man—who was picking up his son after school—first began his tirade, I was afraid my friend was going to have to call security. But within just a few minutes, he had convinced him that his son's punishment was warranted and that, indeed, it was best that the school administer it. He did so in part by enlisting the student's help. He had the boy explain to his dad what he'd done wrong and why this justified his exclusion from the pageant. Hearing his son's explanation made things clear for the man in a way that no amount of explaining from his teacher could have done.

I marveled at my friend's ability to size up the situation and make the right move so smoothly and gracefully. How did he know that it would have been a mistake to engage the father in debate? How did he know that the right thing to do was to enlist the son's assistance? It seemed to me as if he could literally *see* something I couldn't see. He had an ability—as do other people with practical wisdom—to perceive the right thing to do in a way that usually escapes most of us.

But talk of *perceiving* right and wrong may strike us as rather strange. Moral properties aren't like trees or cars; they're not something we can reach out and touch or see or hear. It's not as if right and wrong, good and bad, just and unjust are palpable features of existence, just waiting for us to stumble across. Ongoing disagreement over the morality of everything from abortion to zoos demonstrates that moral properties, whatever they are, don't make themselves readily apparent.

This is true. But difficulty in seeing something doesn't mean it doesn't exist. If it did, then we'd have to deny the existence of subatomic particles or, for that matter, the broad appeal of tractor pulls. Moral properties can be hard to see; they can be difficult to settle on; they can reflect something about the perspective of the person perceiving them. But this doesn't necessarily mean they aren't real.

We just have to understand them in a particular way—a way that will be familiar to anyone who has ever looked through a prism or stood beneath a rainbow.

Relating to Value

When we gaze upon a beautiful sunset and perceive its brilliant reds, oranges, yellows, and purples, our perception is a product of two interrelated factors: first, something about the external physical world—the physics of light, atmosphere, diffusion, and so on—and second, something about our internal mental processes—our eyesight, visual processing systems, sense of perspective, and so on.

Because our experience of the sunset's colors are dependent on the interplay of both these factors, we can say that colors are *relational properties*. That is, in order for them to be perceived, there has to be a relation occurring—the relation between the external physical world and our internal mental process. Obviously, lots of properties are relational properties: sounds, sensations like heat and cold, flavors, and smells.

Understanding moral properties as relational properties doesn't commit us to the objectionable position that any moral view is as good as any other. Just because a property is relational doesn't mean that anything goes.

Consider the analogy with color. Take, for instance, the color of a freshly hewn lawn on a bright summer's day. It's green. That's a matter of fact, even though the fact is dependent upon the interplay of light and the eyesight of the viewer. If someone were to say to us, "Oh. What a lovely red lawn!" we'd think there was something amiss. Either she had a very strange view of the grass, or there was something out of order with her viewing system. Having determined which of these were the case, we could then assist her to see the right color by either changing her view externally or by changing her viewpoint internally. We wouldn't have to simply say, "Oh. Red. That's very interesting. For you it's red, for me it's green. I guess we're both right." We can, quite clearly, recognize that mistakes can be made, and often these mistakes are correctable.

The same goes for moral properties when we understand them as relational properties—at least, the following example makes *me* think so.

My first "real job" is as a ticket seller for a major legitimate theater in San Francisco. I process season ticket subscription orders for shows by touring companies of Broadway's best, including "Evita," "Chorus Line," "Annie," and a revival of "Guys and Dolls." After a couple of seasons of administrative work, I am given the additional opportunity to manage sales of souvenir programs. Before each performance and during intermission, I set up a booth in the lobby and sell glossy keepsakes packed with photos of the casts and sets. It is all on commission, but the money is pretty good. Programs go for $2.50 and I buy them for $2.00. It isn't hard to sell 100 programs a night, which means 50 bucks for a couple hours work—not bad, especially for a 22-year old kid in 1979.

One night, I don't have any quarters for change, so I decide to sell the programs for $3.00. To my surprise, it doesn't seem to make any difference in how fast they move. I decide, after that, to keep the higher price. Why not? I am still paying my distributor his price, nobody is forcing customers to buy, and I am making twice as much. I can't see anything wrong with the arrangement.

It takes about three weeks for me to get caught. One night, the theater's house manager watches me in action. I think she is more surprised that I don't try to hide what I am doing than she is at the inflated price I am charging.

The next day, I am summarily fired. "For what?" I want to know. As far as I can see, I haven't done anything wrong. "Everyone's getting paid, aren't they?"

My boss, in a final gesture of compassion for his terminated employee, helps me see what I've been missing. "In the first place, it's not just the money you owe your distributor. You have an agreement with them that you are not fulfilling. In the second place, as an employee of our theaters, you have a responsibility to us that you are breaking when you fail to offer our customers the best value on their money. Third, you're cheating our customers. And fourth, I warned you not to be greedy when you took this job."

I don't come to perceive the wrongness of my behavior right away. It isn't until a few years later, when I have my own consulting business for which I occasionally hire free-lance people that I really come to appreciate the unacceptability of what I have done. Business relationships are based on trust and when that trust is undermined, the entire system is threatened. The interesting thing is, having improved my perspective on the situation, my response to my behavior becomes more sophisticated as well. Whereas originally I couldn't even tell what all the fuss was about, I now come to have the sort of visceral response one has to morally objectionable behaviors: I feel bad about what I'd done.

So what happened? I believe that a better perspective on the issue allowed me to perceive the wrongness of the act—a perception that, given my limited perspective beforehand, I'd been unable to have. The wrongness was there to be seen all along but only for someone in the proper relation to it. We won't see the beauty, for instance, in a painting by Hans Hoffman unless we take in the whole picture. But it's still there. We won't hear the harmony in a symphony by Mahler unless we hear all the instruments. But it's still there. Similarly, we won't perceive the morality of life's more complex situations unless we stand in the right relationship to what we are perceiving. And that means taking into account as broad a perspective as possible and allowing our sensibilities to operate with as much information as is available.

Only then can we perceive all the colors of the moral spectrum. And only then can we really choose the right thing to do.

The Promise of Perception

Professional philosophers can—and will!—engage in endless debates over the appropriateness of the analogy between moral properties and relational properties like color. Those of us less interested in establishing academic reputations than in improving our ability to perceive and choose the right thing to do, however, can still profit from the analogy—even if it turns out that the folks in the ivory tower have questions left unanswered.

From a practical standpoint, there are a number of benefits that make a strong case for the analogy between moral properties as relational properties. These include the following:

- First, the analogy enables us to make a good case for the reasonable objectivity of moral properties. Our sympathy for diverse viewpoints doesn't back us into the corner of an "anything goes" relativism. On the other hand, since right and wrong *are* a product of a relationship between the judgment and the judged, there is room for a healthy appreciation of individual differences. We're not, in other words, committed to an intolerant moral absolutism.

- Second, the analogy allows us to recognize that moral progress is possible. We can see how mistaken judgments are made and that such judgments can be improved upon. Comparisons can be made, for example, to the world before the invention of the microscope. At that time, people had no tools for seeing microscopic creatures and, consequently, made inaccurate judgments regarding the causes of disease. Following Leeuwenhoek's invention, however, scientists were able to perceive entities they'd previously been unable to and, as a result, were able to make improved judgments—many of which we still accept today. Similarly, in the moral realm, when people don't have the tools needed for perceiving the rightness or wrongness of something, they make judgments that are less accurate than they would be if they had such tools. We can see then, for instance, how the limited perspective of some people in 19th-century America led them to conclude that racism was acceptable and how our wider perspective these days enables us to recognize how horribly mistaken that earlier judgment was.

- Third, the analogy gives us a framework for improving our own—and others'—ability to perceive and choose the right thing to do. If moral properties are something we perceive, then our perceptions can be improved. Compare it to the sensibilities of great painters or great chefs who, through practice, have elevated their abilities to make finer distinctions of color and taste. As "moral artists" we can teach ourselves and each other to make finer moral judgments, too.

- Finally, the analogy encourages us to keep broadening our perspective on the moral issues we face in our personal and professional lives. The promise of improving our judgments in the face of new perspectives compels us to continually reevaluate where we stand on the issues. This increases our potential for making better choices and reduces the likelihood that we will become locked in to a view that no longer reflects our current values and vision for the people we hope to be.

So How Does It Work, Already?

I've suggested that an understanding of what I'm calling the *moral spectrum* model has real-world benefits, not only in the realm of the moral judgments we make but for other aspects of our lives as well.

So, how does it work? What's involved in *perceiving* the right thing to do? How are we to use the so-called moral spectrum model to improve our ability to make the best choices possible? Suppose moral properties *are* like colors; how does the moral spectrum model enable us to see them more clearly?

These questions and more will be addressed in Chapter 2, "The Moral Spectrum." So, if you're interested in the answers, then you may find that the right thing to do is keep reading.

The Moral Spectrum

Broadening Our Perspective on the Right Thing to Do

How Do You Know What's Right?

Recently you made a moral decision. You faced a situation with moral import and decided what was the right thing to do. (This doesn't necessarily mean you *did* what was right; you may have, for a variety of reasons, done quite the opposite.) It may have been a question of minor importance: whether to tip a waiter at a restaurant to which you'll never return. Or it may have been one of far greater consequence: how to care for an aging relative in the last few months of his or her life.

Regardless of the weight of the question, you probably employed some principle in answering it. You probably used some guidelines for determining the most appropriate course of action. You probably appealed to something beyond the particular facts of the situation at hand, something that *determined* what was the right and wrong thing to do. In this sense, you engaged in moral reasoning. You turned your attention away from the particular moral question at hand: What *is* the right thing to do? You focused instead on the more theoretical question: What *makes* it the right thing to do? By doing so, however, you were able to solve the practical problem and come to the decision you needed to make. Such appeals to principle, to guidelines, to something beyond the situation at hand are standard features of our moral practice. Without them, our moral decisions would essentially be *ad hoc*. And lacking any consistency, they'd hardly be considered moral.

However, despite the importance of these principles to making wise moral decisions, we're often unaware of what they are. This is in part because we've so internalized them. We don't have to be conscious of how we're coming to moral conclusions to come to them. Like skilled athletes who don't have to think about how to play the game, we too can *just do it* when determining what's right and what's wrong.

Nevertheless, if we examine the manner in which we arrive at our moral conclusions, we can increase the likelihood that those conclusions will consistently reflect our deepest, most abiding values. Even the world's best athletes are constantly reevaluating their swings, strides, and shots in an effort to improve upon them. They know that the more conscious they are of what makes them succeed, the more they'll be able to make the adjustments necessary to keep them at the top of their games.

The same goes for those of us who want to do the best we can at choosing the right thing to do. Examining the manner in which we make such choices enables us to continually improve upon them. Looking "beneath the hood" of our particular moral judgments allows us to tune up the machinery that generates those judgments.

Most of us spend plenty of time looking in the mirror to enhance the outward appearance of the person who stares back at us; shouldn't we spend a comparable amount of time reflecting on our internal characters in order to make them more attractive as well?

The first step, then, is to hold up the mirror. We can then look into it by considering the way we typically make moral decisions. The principles and guidelines that are reflected back will help us see what's at the foundation of our particular choices—and indeed, if those choices are the ones that, on reflection, we would still be happy to make.

Horns of the Dilemma

All of us have, at one time or another, faced a moral dilemma. We've experienced the troubling nature of the question: damned if I do and damned if I don't. Somehow though, we've made a decision—and the way we have says a lot about who we are.

The 20th-century existentialist philosopher Jean-Paul Sartre describes the following moral dilemma. During World War II, a young French student faces a choice between leaving his village to join the Resistance forces or staying home to care for his aged, infirm mother. His brother has been killed by the Germans, so he feels it is his duty to avenge the death. But his mother is wholly dependent on his support; if he leaves, she will be plunged into despair and will probably die. According to Sartre, there is no principle on which to decide this matter; the young man must simply choose. No rule of general morality can show us what we ought to do in the world; we are free and must invent ourselves through our choices.

While no one would deny that Sartre's student faces a difficult choice, not everyone would agree that there is no principle to which the young man can appeal. Most of us, were we in such situation, would use some sort of criterion to tell us what to do. We might, for instance, try to figure out which choice would lead to less unhappiness. We would decide what to do based on whether our mother or our country would suffer more from our absence. Or we might rely on a rule that we believe ought not to be violated at any cost—say, honor one's father and mother. We might think of the most virtuous person we know and try to imagine what he or she would do. Or we might, not unlike Sartre, say that the best way to choose is simply to "trust our gut." But if we did, unlike Sartre, we'd be appealing to a principle—one that basically says, "When facing moral dilemmas, trust your gut."

We can see this more clearly when we think of the more common sort of dilemmas we regularly face in our personal and professional lives. Many of us, for example, confront a dilemma in caring for our children: Should we work longer hours to provide them with material advantages even though it means spending less time together? Or should we forego career opportunities to have more time with them, although this means they won't have all the neat stuff that their friends do? To solve this dilemma, most of us will sit down and reason it in some way; we'll weigh the pros and cons and eventually come up with a decision. What's particularly interesting though—and what Sartre's analysis of our moral decision-making process *does* capture—is that our final decision may *not* bear a direct relationship to the decision we made by weighing the pros and cons. Often, as a matter of fact, our final decision is the opposite of our reasoned decision. But this doesn't mean that there's no relationship between the reasoning and the final course of action. It's like flipping a coin to decide what to do, and when heads comes up we suddenly realize that what we really want to do is tails. The process of reasoning serves to jump-start our intuition so we can arrive at a decision that best reflects our deepest values.

Many of us had similar experiences with moral dilemmas on the job. My friend Dennis, who's a general contractor, told me about a carpenter he knows about who insists on being paid in cash. The guy obviously does so to avoid paying taxes on his income. But he passes his savings along to his customers, so there's an incentive to play along. Plus, he does excellent work.

Dennis decided not to use him even though it meant he would have to charge his own clients a bit more. He said, "Look, here's a case where the benefits of working with the guy obviously outweigh the disadvantages. I mean, think of how glad my customers are gonna be to save a couple hundred bucks. And who's *really* gonna notice if this guy doesn't pay his taxes? It's not gonna impact the national debt, that's for sure. Still, the thing is, I think of the effect of *my* choice to work with him and I think: 'Suppose everybody chose like me—what sort of people would those be?' Not ones I want to be associated with, anyway. So, I'm sorry, no dice for this carpenter."

Here Dennis is weighing several principles against one another. He realizes that, ultimately, people would be happier if he worked with the carpenter; so if the principle is "maximize happiness," he ought to. But he balances that against something like a principle of universalizability: don't do things that, if everyone did them, would make for a world you would find unacceptable. Choosing between these principles is, for Dennis, a matter of intuition; one of them just feels right.

Examining the way a person resolves moral dilemmas provides insight into his or her decision-making process. And when it's *our own* process we're examining, the insight is even more telling.

I was trying to decide whether to include a fairly personal story in this book about a friend of mine. It didn't represent her in the most flattering of lights, but it did illustrate very well a point I wanted to make. I asked her what she thought. She said she preferred I didn't use it but that, ultimately, it was up to me. After all, *I* was the one writing a book about moral choices; shouldn't I know the right thing to do?

After some soul-searching, I decided not to include the story. It seemed to me that the pain I would cause my friend by doing so outweighed any benefits to potential readers. I tried to put myself in my friend's shoes: How would *I* feel if she did something like that to me? Plus, I tried to imagine how I would regard myself if I included it. Wouldn't I feel like a traitor or at least like someone whose priorities were a bit skewed?

Examining the way I came to the conclusion I did helped me see some of the criteria I was using to determine the right thing to do. And it got me thinking about the various considerations we all tend to appeal to when faced with difficult moral choices.

Considering the Considerations

When trying to figure out the right thing to do, people generally appeal to a variety of considerations that can be broken down as follows:

- *Feelings vs. Principles*: People either tend to rely on their emotions or to consciously consider rules when making moral decisions. Some try to "get a feel" for the issue; they trust their moral sensibilities to tell them what to do. Others use their heads more than their hearts; they rely on reason to be the guide about what makes something the right or wrong thing to do.

- *Motives vs. Outcomes:* People tend to be more concerned with either the motives underlying a choice or the outcomes that follow from it. Some concentrate on *why* a person is choosing as he or she is; they want to make sure that the reasons for a particular decision are morally praiseworthy. Others look at the consequences of a particular choice; they want to make sure that valuable ends are attained by a particular attitude or behavior.

- *Individual vs. Societal Considerations*: In determining the right thing to do, people tend to refer either to their own moral intuitions or to the more generally accepted societal declarations of right and wrong. It's a question of individual character or societal character. Some concentrate on the type of person they will become as a result of making a given choice; they are interested in the type of person who is reflected by their morality. Others turn their attention to the sort of society they are manifesting through their decisions; their interest is more on what a group of people who choose as they do are saying about themselves.

Each of these pairs of considerations represents a spectrum along which our decision-making process may fall. We may think

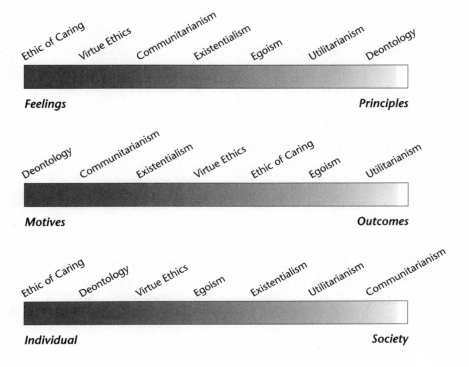

Feelings — Principles

Motives — Outcomes

Individual — Society

of these spectra as *moral spectra*, along which we can locate some of the better-known moral theories in Western philosophy.

These seven theories can—at a general level—be understood as approaching the resolution of moral issues by appealing more or less to feelings or principles, motives or outcomes, individual or societal effects. Briefly, we can characterize each of these seven theories as follows:

- *Existentialism:* Existentialism, that much-misunderstood and often-parodied 20th-century philosophy, offers its own way to think about right and wrong. Basically, existentialists deny that there is any objective meaning to be found in the universe. It is incumbent upon each of us to determine the meaning of our own lives. Human beings have no "essence" apart from what we choose it to be. There are no principles in nature that will tell us how we ought to behave. Existentialism is thus often misunderstood as saying there is no right or wrong; anything goes. Jean-Paul Sartre, existentialism's most famous proponent, however, offers a profound admonition to guide our choices. Since there are no objective principles in the universe, each of us must realize that, in any choice we make, we are implicitly choosing for all of humanity. When I say, for instance, that I should not steal CDs from my local record store, I am saying no one should. The awesome responsibility that this places on each of us every time we make a choice is the source of our deep existential anguish. But the realization that we are completely free to choose what's right and what's wrong involves a recognition that freedom is the foundation for all values. Thus, says Sartre, actions of people of good faith have, as their ultimate significance, the quest of such freedom.[3] Enlarging the realm of human freedom becomes our guiding principle. An existentialist ethic will therefore filter the world through the maximization of people's liberty. The right thing to do will be the choice that best expresses and sustains the enlargement of the realm of human freedom—the choice that sets people most free.

- *Deontology:* Deontology is "duty-based" ethics. This is the moral theory of the 18th-century philosopher, Immanuel Kant. According to Kant, an action is morally worthy only if it is undertaken out of a sense of moral duty. The principle that underlies morally worthy actions is what Kant calls the "categorical imperative." Basically, the categorical imperative says that we should behave only in ways that we would be willing to have everyone else in the world behave in. It's the general principle with which we are all familiar: if you

---

[3]Sartre, Jean-Paul, "Existentialism is a Humanism," in *Existentialism and Humanism* (London: Methuen and Co, Ltd., 1948).

wouldn't want everyone else to act in a certain way, then you shouldn't either.

- *An Ethic of Caring:* A number of contemporary feminist philosophers, notably Nel Noddings and Carol Gilligan, have developed a moral theory in which the right thing to do is to be found through an emphasis on the relationship of caring between human beings. This theory explicitly rejects the long-standing emphasis in morality on principles, reason, and judgment. "An ethic of caring," says Nodding, "locates morality primarily in the pre-act consciousness of the one-caring."[4] Right and wrong emerge in light of an ethical ideal, a vision of our best self. This best self is who we are—or who we remember being—in those moments when we experience the sentiment of natural caring such as parents feel for their children. So, when trying to decide the right thing to do, we must focus on the particulars of the situation at hand and try to behave in a manner consistent with this best self, one that maintains and enhances the caring relationship between ourselves as the one-caring and others as the ones cared-for.

- *Communitarianism:* Communitarianism, which currently is experiencing newfound interest among educators and social policy-makers, is informed by—among other things—the moral theory of 18th-century British philosopher David Hume. According to Hume, our judgments of right and wrong are a matter of spreading our feelings over the world. As members of a community, we enact rules that reflect these feelings. To do the right thing, therefore, is to follow these rules and, in doing so, express our moral sensibilities through our choices. Assessing the rightness or wrongness of someone's actions is a matter of assessing someone's motives for the choices they make. Consider how different our judgment of

---

[4]Noddings, Nel, *Caring: A Feminine Approach to Ethics and Moral Education* (Berkeley: University of California Press, 1984), p. 28.

Robin Hood— who robs from the rich to give to the poor—is from our judgment of the Sheriff of Nottingham—who does just the opposite—and you'll see what Hume means. It turns in large part on people's motives; if their reasons for behaving a certain way are admirable, we're likely to judge their actions as admirable, too.

- *Utilitarianism*: Utilitarianism was developed by the 19th-century English philosopher Jeremy Bentham and expanded by his pupil and colleague John Stuart Mill. According to Mill, an action is right insofar as it maximizes total *utility*, where utility is generally reckoned as the sum of total pleasure over pain. To determine if something is the right thing to do or not, we calculate how much pleasure and how much pain will be generated by doing it; if the consequences lead to more pleasure and less pain—not just for ourselves, but for everyone everywhere—then the action is morally justified.

- *Virtue Ethics:* Virtue ethics has its roots in the moral theory of Aristotle. According to Aristotle, virtuous acts are those performed by a virtuous person. To become a virtuous person, we must undergo the proper training of our feeling and attitudes. Having done so (assuming our character is of the right sort), we will take pleasure in virtuous action. We will consistently choose the mean between the vice of excess and the vice of deficiency and so will manifest courage, temperance, friendliness, and other moral virtues in our choices.

- *Egoism:* Ethical egoism is the view that the right thing to do is whatever best succeeds in helping us achieve our rationally chosen ends. The 18th-century philosopher and political theorist Adam Smith, for instance, argues that a kind of rational self-interest should be the determining factor in what makes right acts right. Thomas Hobbes, whose moral theory is also based in egoism, reminds us that the best way for people to escape the "solitary, nasty, brutish, and short" state of nature in which everyone is continually at war with everyone else, is to establish self-interested convenants with one another. People should act egoistically—that is, they ought to try to maximize the benefits to themselves—and in doing so, will maximize the common good. An egoist ethics filters the world through people's reasonable desires. When trying to figure out the right thing to do, egoists ask themselves what choice would best help them get what they really want. (And presumably, since very few egoists want to go to prison, very few would do just *anything*.) The "invisible hand" coordinating human interactions will then ensure that as each of us egoistically pursues our own individual goals, our common goals—peace, stability, abundance—are likewise achieved.

These seven theories do not constitute an exhaustive list of all the ways people might possibly determine the right thing to do. They do, however, define a range of possibilities along the three continuums: Feelings/Principles, Motives/Outcomes, and Individual/Societal Considerations. While there's certainly room for discussion about *exactly* where any theory lies along a particular scale, we can easily see that different theories stress different criteria for determining right and wrong. Compare, for instance, the explicit rejection of principles on the part of an ethic of caring to the single-minded focus that utilitarians place on the utilitarian principle. Or notice how important motives are to a deontologist in determining the right thing to do as compared to how critical outcomes are to a utilitarian. Or contrast how an ethic of caring locates the core of morality in an individual's response to a particular situation with how communitarianism determines right and wrong in light of a shared perception on the part of social groups.

Because these seven theories do span such a broad array of possible approaches across the three spectra under consideration, they provide for a virtually unlimited number of combinations to explore when trying to develop a nuanced perception of how we ought to behave. In the same way that the seven colors of the visible spectrum (remember your colorful friend, ROY G. BIV)—red, orange, yellow, green, blue, indigo, violet—make possible an incalculable number of shades and hues, so the seven "colors" in the moral spectrum (think of your ethical friend, ED C. CUVE)—existentialism, deontology, an ethic of caring, communitarianism, utilitarianism, virtue ethics, and egoism—give us an incredibly rich palette of possibilities for perceiving, and ultimately choosing, the right thing to do.

A Richer Palette, a Sharper Prism

The previous brief discussion of moral theory is in no way meant to capture the intricacies of the theories discussed. Rather, it is primarily intended to help us identify the various ways in which most of us tend to go about making moral choices.

We can think of each of the perspectives as a kind of prism. When you hold a prism up to the light, it breaks what's invisible into all the colors of the rainbow. The prism allows you to see the full spectrum of colors that make up each ray of light. In a similar manner, the moral perspective you take on a particular issue enables you to see what had been invisible to you before: its ethical dimension. And, as with a prism, the colors you see depend on the perspective you take. It's not as if you're seeing something that isn't there, but it is the case that unless you put the prism up to your eyes, you won't see it.

If you think about how you usually determine what you ought to do, you'll probably find that you generally incline toward one— or maybe two—of the seven moral theories we've looked at. You'll probably find that you usually ask yourself a characteristic question associated with that particular theory. It is useful, therefore, both as a way to clarify your own perspective and to prepare for expanding your moral palette, to have in mind the central question each of the perspectives asks when assessing an issue. What, in other words, is the prism through which each perspective views the world?

Imagine that you are considering whether something is the right or wrong thing to do. The way you question yourself provides a pretty good guide for which one (or more) of the seven prisms you are using.

- The existentialist prism asks:
  "What course(s) of action will set people most free?"

- The deontological prism asks:
  "What would I do if everyone in the world were to do as I did?"

- The ethic of caring prism asks:
  "What course(s) of action will best sustain and nurture a caring relationship between myself and others?"

- The communitarian prism asks:
  "How would I act if everyone in my community knew exactly what I were doing?"

- The utilitarian prism asks:
  "What course(s) of action will best maximize total happiness in the world?"

- The virtue ethics prism asks:
  "What would the most virtuous person I know of do in this situation?"

- The egoist prism asks:
  "What course(s) of action will most effectively ensure that my short- and long-term goals are reached?"

The way to use the moral spectrum model is, in keeping with the many-hued theme, as a palette. When considering a moral issue, most of us tend to paint with a limited number of colors. Using the moral spectrum model enables us to expand our palette and see different perspectives that we can then bring to the issue. For instance, if we generally gaze through the deontological prism, we're apt to be focused less on results than on motives, which may lead us to making choices that underplay their effect on people's happiness. It may be worth our while, therefore, to gaze through the utilitarian prism and see if our judgment of what we ought to do changes. Considering the issue from this new point of view won't necessarily change our mind, but it will bring new options to the table.

In short, the moral spectrum model enables us to expand our moral perception and with any luck, choose more wisely.

The first step in doing so, then, is to identify which of the seven prisms you tend to rely on. You can then expand your moral palette by blending in the perspectives you tend to downplay.

Your Own Moral Prism

Recall how my friend Dennis solved the dilemma about whether to hire the carpenter who worked only for cash. He based his decision on a principle that says not to do things you wouldn't want everyone else to do. He considered what would happen if everyone modeled their behavior on his choice. So, he's pretty obviously deciding from the deontological perspective; we can say that his moral prism refracts the deontological perspective.

Or reflect back on one way of solving the dilemma Sartre's student faced. Suppose you said that he ought to care for his aged mother because she would suffer so much if he didn't. And you might add, one should always follow the rule that says, "minimize suffering whenever possible." Here then, you'd be considering consequences, specifically, the unhappiness the student's mother would experience versus the unhappiness the student or potential Resistance fighters would feel. Clearly, you'd be looking through the utilitarian moral prism.

Determining the moral prism you usually employ is a matter of reflecting on choices you have made—or are making—observing the kinds of questions you ask yourself, and identifying which prism(s) you are employing.

Of course, few of us *always* choose from a single perspective. Most people shift around, depending on the circumstances. With our families, since we're particularly interested in their pleasure, we may tend to be more utilitarian. On the job, we're apt to be more focused on motives and principles, and so may come from a more deontological perspective.

Still, nearly everyone has a preferred mode of operating. In the contemporary United States, for example, most people are utilitarian of some stripe. Our heritage of majority rule tends to make us see right and wrong in terms of what makes the most people happy or unhappy. The next most common prism is probably deontology. Many people, especially those with a strong religious heritage, are quite focused on particular moral duties and judge accordingly. The virtue ethics perspective is also often employed by individuals with strong feelings for religion. The question, "What Would Jesus Do?" is a way of thinking about how the most virtuous person they know of would act. Another not uncommon prism is the communitarian perspective. Young people especially tend to see morality as mainly a matter of social convention; right and wrong are determined by one's community and that's all there is to it. The existentialist perspective is probably used more often by young people—especially teenagers—than adults. When we are still experimenting with lifestyle and values, we tend to put a premium on the freedom to express ourselves. An ethic of caring is less frequently used; it is more often viewed as a way for parents to meet the needs of their children than as a strategy for dealing with moral issues outside the home. Finally, egoism, while often held up as an economic ideal, does not generally enjoy such popularity in the moral arena. Still, the egoist perspective, especially if it is tempered by one or more of the other prisms, does represent a manner in which some people will typically choose the right thing to do.

When we think about how we usually decide what we ought or ought not to do, most of us will probably realize that we do tend to favor one perspective over another. Most of us have a characteristic moral prism through which we view the world. It's apparent, therefore, that we can benefit from expanding our moral palette by learning to take into account the other perspectives.

To do so, we need to familiarize ourselves with each of the seven moral prisms. The following stories are intended to help us do so by, in part, highlighting some of each prism's strengths and weaknesses.

The Existentialist Prism

"What course(s) of action will set people most free?"

In 1979, TWA was having a contest in which you could win a free round-trip ticket to any destination they served. There were two ways to enter: you could buy a ticket on the airline, or send in a self-addressed stamped envelope and receive a game ticket by return mail. The regulations said that a person could request only one entry per day. To circumvent that constraint, I had everyone I knew address envelopes for me. I realized that I was breaking the rules, but I didn't care; any guilt I might have felt was mitigated by having a mailbox full of scratch-off sweepstakes entries waiting for me every day when I returned from work.

One day I arrived home to find my girlfriend Rita excitedly waving a game ticket at me. "You won! You won!" she cried.

I was too delighted by my good fortune to be upset that she'd not only opened my mail but had also scratched off my entries. I took the winning ducat from her and began fantasizing about how I'd use it. The round-trip permitted two stopovers, so I would fly to Paris, then to Athens, then to Moscow before returning home—if I returned home at all. With 12 months to complete my travel, anything could happen.

As I waxed rhapsodic about my upcoming adventure, I didn't notice Rita's face turning darker and darker. Suddenly, she snatched the ticket out of my hand. "I can't believe you think you're going to go flying all over the world without me! Well, forget it! This ticket came in an envelope addressed to Looey!"

Looey was my roommate, co-worker, and best friend. We had been living together for about six months.

"Don't be ridiculous," I said. "It's my ticket. Looey just addressed the envelope. I asked him to. He knows it's mine."

"Yeah? Well, why don't you ask him yourself?"

As if on cue, Looey walked in the door. Rita rushed over to him with the winning game card. "Look what came in the mail for you today!"

"All right," deadpanned Looey, checking out the scratched-off stub. "Morocco here I come."

"That's mine and you know it," I said.

"Rita said it came in an envelope addressed to me."

"But *I* was the one who asked you to address it. You knew you were addressing it for me!"

"I did? That's news."

"That's bullshit!" I cried and snatched the ticket away from him. Then, before he could grab it back, I ran into my room and locked it in my desk.

"We'll see whose ticket it is," I announced, returning to the living room.

"Yeah," replied Looey. "We will."

Over the course of the next few days, everyone we knew divided into a Looey camp or a David camp. Our entire office was split down the middle. You couldn't take a break without hearing co-workers arguing about who really had a right to the ticket.

Looey and I tried not to get too caught up in it, but it wasn't easy. Our friendship was strained and tested as it had never been before.

For some reason, though, we seemed to hit on the same strategy for dealing with it: avoidance. Rather than working toward a solution, we just pretended there wasn't a problem. As the weeks went by, we acted pretty much as we always did—riding the bus together to work, eating lunch at the same restaurant, having a few beers at our local watering hole at quitting time. Meanwhile, the winning sweepstakes ticket remained locked in my desk.

As it turned out, the right thing to do emerged by examining things through the existentialist moral prism. We were sitting at one of our usual lunchtime hangouts, an Italian restaurant called *Original Joe's,* when it dawned on us what we ought to do.

"You know, I don't really care about going to Morocco," said Looey. "I'd just like to get out of town for a few days."

"And to tell you the truth," I admitted. "I just like the idea of having the resources to go somewhere sometime if I want to. Like money in the bank."

We decided that there was a way in which both of our desires could be liberated: if we found someone who was planning on taking a trip anyway, we could sell them the ticket and split the money. Moreover, their freedom to travel would be maximized, too, since we could sell them our winning stub for cheaper than they could purchase their airfare.

So that's what we did. Our mutual friend, Larry, was getting ready to tour England and Scandinavia. A regular fare ticket to the destinations he had in mind would cost $1200.00. We sold him the game ticket for $800.00. Looey went to Reno for a weekend. I put the money in my savings and used it to help me move to L.A. a few months later.

In this case, the right thing to do was determined by an action that gave all of us involved the greatest possible range of free choice. Looey was able to express his wish to get out of town, I was able to realize my goal of having a kind of financial safety-net, and, Larry, by saving some money, was given the freedom to extend his tour a little longer. This maximization of freedom is in keeping with the ideal of the existentialist prism—and highlights both some of its strengths and a few of its weaknesses.

On the plus side, the existentialist prism recognizes the critical connection between liberty and justice. As a general rule, whatever maximizes people's autonomy is also whatever's most fair.

Moreover, because the existentialist prism is based in Sartre's contention that, when we make choices, we are implicitly choosing for all of humanity, it reminds us that we should choose wisely and with regard to the legacy we are leaving. The only moral truths are human moral truths, and only our actions, not our words, are evidence for them. So it is incumbent upon each of us to take action that maximizes human freedom and, in doing so, create a moral legacy of which we can individually and collectively be proud.

On the minus side, though, it's not obvious that we should always hold freedom as our highest ideal. Lots of times, the right thing to do seems to require that we constrain people's liberty—especially if those people are children and the highest expression of their liberty would involve say, playing in traffic or with sharp knives. Freedom is a worthy goal, but certainly not the *only* one. Compassion, honesty, and safety, among others, may sometimes provide us with a better guide to what we ought to do.

We should also question Sartre's contention that our choices always reflect the manner in which we believe all humanity should behave. As Nel Noddings reminds us, the particular features of our lives are unique. It's a mistake to abstract away from the particulars in an attempt to universalize our experience. The right thing to do is sometimes right precisely because it does take into account the uniqueness of each situation. The existentialist prism may lead us to overlook the special relationships between people in particular situations. Also, since it is focused so heavily on active expression, it has a tendency to run roughshod over people's feelings, especially people who are reticent to expose them. Given this, it seems apparent that our moral choices will be wiser if we use one or more of the other perspectives in conjunction with the existentialist moral prism.

The Deontological Moral Prism

"What would I do if everyone in the world were to do as I did?"

My wife, my best friend Harley, and I were in Las Vegas—admittedly, not the first place in the world that comes to mind when one thinks of moral behavior. We were in a casino downtown playing some slots, some craps, and having a few drinks. As is not uncommon in Vegas, a stranger approached and started talking to us as if we had known him all our lives. And before we knew it—as is often not uncommon in Vegas—we all felt like we did.

We were drinking, laughing, sharing our slot machines, having a grand old time. That's when the stranger, who we now knew by the name of Kenny, proposed we go to another casino and play poker. Harley, Jen, and I were hesitant; for one thing, none of us was very good at cards. It didn't seem like a fun prospect to go and sit in a room with a bunch of cigar-chomping card sharks who would probably fleece us of our gambling stake.

But Kenny assured us that this isn't what would happen. His friend was a dealer, he said. He could rig it so we would be certain of being dealt winning hands. All we would have to do is slip him a small percentage of our take. It was a sure thing, no strings attached.

I wondered out loud why Kenny himself didn't take advantage of this opportunity. Why was he turning us on to his friend instead of putting some money in his own pocket?

Kenny said he couldn't do that because they knew him at the casino. He'd already won too much and had been barred from playing there. But we were new in town; we could win plenty before anyone got wise.

Harley and I thought it sounded like a good deal. What did we have to lose? After all, even if Kenny's friend didn't come through and we lost our money, we'd be no worse off than we would normally. And if he did come through, we'd be sitting pretty. So why not go for it?

We were just about to head to the other casino with Kenny when Jennifer posed a question that made us reconsider our decision. "What would happen," she asked, "if everyone cheated like this?"

"That's the beauty part," said Kenny. "Everyone doesn't. It's only the suckers who don't cheat. And you guys aren't suckers."

"But *what if* everyone cheated? What would happen?"

"I guess it would be the end of Vegas," I said. "There wouldn't be any games if nobody played the game."

"Exactly," said Jen. "And so where would we be?"

"In the middle of the desert with not much to do," said Harley.

I concurred. "Yeah, not where I'd want to be."

At this point, our interest in going with Kenny to the other casino essentially evaporated. And so, in a few minutes, did Kenny. He couldn't understand why we were being such suckers. And suckers weren't the kind of people he wanted to be friends with.

But I don't think we were being suckers. We were just being good Kantians, looking through the deontological moral prism and asking ourselves whether we could reasonably universalize our actions. We wondered what would happen if everyone behaved like us. And we concluded that, by doing so, we'd land ourselves in a blatant contradiction: we'd be trying to cheat in a world where cheating couldn't exist. It would be like saying (to use one of Kant's examples), "I am going to break a promise in a world where there is no such thing as promising." But that's irrational. And since, for Kant, we have a duty as rational beings to behave rationally, it is—broadly—immoral to be irrational. As the deontological moral prism tell us, it is immoral to act in ways that we couldn't reasonably be willing to have everyone else act. So, in our case, it would have been wrong for us to take Kenny up on his offer to cheat at poker with his friendly dealer.

Kant's first version of the ultimate moral principle, his so-called "categorical imperative," says that we must act only in ways whereby the "maxim" (something like the motive) of our action could at the same time be made universal law. We have to be able to imagine a world in which everyone did as we do; if in such a world, our motive contradicts itself (like willing to cheat in a world with no cheating, or to promise in a world without promises), then the action we're considering is wrong. If the motive isn't contradictory (like willing to not cheat in a world where cheating is possible), then it's morally acceptable.

This principle, along with the example above, reveals some of the strengths and weaknesses of the deontological prism.

On the plus side, deontology provides a clear principle for resolving moral dilemmas. Regardless of what it is, whether it's "Do unto others as you would have them do unto you," or "Never take actions you wouldn't want everyone else to," principle, for deontologists, is paramount. This makes it easy to appeal to principle in the attempt to find answers and resolve disputes. The deontological prism also recognizes the importance of moral duties. Although it's not particularly fashionable anymore to think this way, it has long been agreed that we do have certain moral duties, such as honesty, benevolence, and loyalty. The deontological perspective holds these duties as preeminent and guards against the tendency to downplay them. And, perhaps most important, it attempts to apply a universal standard to all people, everywhere. The principles by which the deontological perspective operates are meant to have universal scope. This holds everyone everywhere to the same standard and protects us against injustices that might seem justified by circumstances or outcomes.

On the other hand, the deontological prism can be overly inflexible. A dyed-in-the-wool deontologist says that we must adhere to our duties, no matter what. Kant is infamous for maintaining that one has a duty not to lie, even if someone's life is at stake. But the world doesn't always seem to work this way; sometimes rules *are* made to be broken.

By the same token, the deontological prism seems to underplay the importance of consequences to our determinations of right and wrong. Again, if all we're focused on is our duties, we can sometimes not achieve the best results. We might, for instance, have a duty to punish wrongdoers, but in certain cases, this would create such unhappiness that punishment would be highly inappropriate.

Finally, the deontological moral prism may be too focused on people as autonomous agents; many of our moral responsibilities, in contrast, have to do with relationships between people. Deontology tends to assume that people have equal opportunities to fulfill their duties. But as we all know, there are mitigating factors that impinge on this. Moreover, some of our duties are based on our not being free agents: duties to our children, for instance. For these reasons and more, we're apt to make wiser moral choices by using the deontological prism in conjunction with one or more of the other six.

The Ethic of Caring Prism

"What course(s) of action will best sustain and nurture a caring relationship between myself and others?"

I was 11 years old when Martin Luther King, Jr., was murdered, but I understood what had happened well enough to weep. I hid in the bottom bunk of my bunkbeds, huddled against the wall, crying into the fur of my teddy bear, whom I had earlier decided I was far too mature for anymore.

My parents were deeply involved in organizing a response to the tragedy. My mother, a past president of the local League of Women Voters, was planning a meeting at the organization's headquarters. My father talked on the phone with fellow physicians who were preparing to respond to the violence that would inevitably result.

Hearing his voice echoing down to my bedroom, I crept silently upstairs to his attic office. He had the telephone cradled in his neck and was quickly jotting down notes on a yellow legal pad. Even through my tears, I could see he was terribly busy, and from the look on his face, I could tell it was something terribly important. I bit my lower lip trying to be brave as, noticing my entrance, his gaze caught mine.

Without hesitation, though, my father spoke a few concluding words into the receiver and hung up. He crossed the room to me and wrapped his arms around my shoulders. We sat on his big easy chair, and my head fell to his chest. I smelled his lemony sweat-smell and the tickly scent of tobacco on his fingers.

He asked me how I was feeling. Was I scared? Yes? He was, too. I raised my head and met his eyes. His were glistening, just like mine. My father tightened his arms around me, and I filled his shirt pocket with tears. Soon I fell asleep, and he carried me down to my room and tucked me in to bed. All that remained of my fear was the wet stain on his pocket.

In this case, my father made the maintenance of the caring relationship between us his highest priority. He chose the right thing to do by asking what course of action would best sustain and nurture the caring relationship between himself and me. This meant he had to set aside other duties to which he was attending, but—given the prism though which he was gazing—those duties paled in comparison.

We can see from this example that one of the great strengths of an ethic of caring is its compassionate nature. Actions deemed appropriate by this moral prism will typically be those that protect and cherish the feelings of others. Using an ethic of caring to determine the right thing to do will usually lead us to make choices that are extremely sensitive to the needs of the people involved in the situation.

This focus on particulars, however, reveals a possible shortcoming in the ethic of caring perspective. Nel Noddings reminds us that an ethic of caring explicitly rejects the notion that moral principles must be universalizable: that is, that they must apply to all sufficiently similar people in sufficiently similar circumstances. The problem with trying to make moral principles universalizable, she argues, is that in doing so, we can't help but abstract away from the concrete facts of the situation at hand that render it problematic. So we have to consider each situation on its own, taking into account the unique features and feelings of the people involved.

The difficulty here is twofold. First, it makes us have to do a lot of work to figure out what we ought to do. Since there are no general principles to appeal to, we have to critically assess each and every situation by examining it quite carefully. This may be time-consuming to say the least and often, in fact, quite impossible.

Second, there is a danger with the ethic of caring of falling prey to relativism. Because right and wrong depend so heavily on the particular features of particular cases, it may turn out that we're unable to condemn an action that we generally deem to be wrong. Noddings herself admits: "The lessons in 'right' and 'wrong' are hard lessons—not swiftly accomplished by setting up as an objective the learning of some principle. We do not say: It is wrong to steal. Rather, we consider why it was wrong or may be wrong in this case to steal. We do not say: It is wrong to kill. By setting up such a principle, we also imply its exceptions, and then we may too easily act on authorized exceptions."[5]

Viewing situations *only* through the ethic of caring prism may cause us to make choices that overemphasize mercy at the expense of justice. (You could imagine a case where a parent, for instance, would be unwilling to punish his or her child, even if that child did something that any reasonable person would say merited redress.) Consequently, as with any of the seven perspectives, we are apt to make more sophisticated choices by using the ethic of caring prism in conjunction with one or more of the others.

The Communitarian Prism

"How would I act if everyone in my community knew exactly what I were doing?"

In a business ethics class I was teaching, we had explored a case study about the allegedly deceptive marketing practices of certain liquor manufacturers. Students were intrigued by the material, and we had a number of very lively discussions about whether it was morally acceptable for companies to sell highly alcoholic "fortified wines" in bottles that resembled low-alcohol wine coolers.

So, I thought that for the last class of the quarter it might be fun to bring in a sample of one of these so-called "wine foolers" for students to sample if they wanted. After all, it was a summer class—where things are pretty casual—and all my students were over 21 years of age.

In thinking about whether I ought to do this or not, I noticed that I was being extremely secretive about my preparations. I was terrified that my faculty advisor would find out what I was up to. I refrained from discussing it with any of my graduate student colleagues. My plan was to sneak the beverages into class, swear my students to secrecy in tasting them, and deny that I had done so if anyone asked me about it.

---

[5]Noddings, op cit., p. 93.

But on my way to the corner store to pick up the drinks, a little light went on in my head. If I were so nervous about being found out, didn't this suggest pretty strongly that I had real reservations about whether I was doing the right thing? After all, nearly every other time in my life that I had tried to hide what I was doing was one in which I knew I was doing what I shouldn't be. Like when I was 8 and tried unsuccessfully to cover up how I was stealing matches from my mom's downstairs "junk drawer" under the guise of getting repeated drinks of water from the kitchen faucet.

By asking myself how I would act if everyone knew what I was doing, I came to the conclusion that I really ought not to bring the alcohol to class. It was perfectly obvious that doing so would violate norms of behavior that were operative in my community. And it was obvious that I was kidding myself if I pretended I didn't know this—or if I tried to convince myself that I didn't think those norms were justified.

We can see here what works and what doesn't about the communitarian perspective. On the positive side, it reminds us that, in some ways, right and wrong are socially constructed. Often, determining the right thing to do is a matter of getting a clearer picture of what our society has to say about the matter. While we want to be careful about saying that culture *defines* right and wrong, the communitarian perspective helps us maintain an awareness of how different societies have at different times held different viewpoints. This enables us to be more open to reflecting upon and improving our own beliefs.

Moreover, the communitarian perspective respects the value of our moral intuitions. Most of us probably have a better-developed sense of right and wrong than we're always aware of. That's why everyone from truck drivers to presidents skulks about when they're doing something they know they shouldn't. It's not as if *everything* that we'd like to keep private about ourselves is something that's morally questionable, but it is the case that nearly all the morally questionable things we do are things we'd like to keep under wraps.

Of course, this also reveals what can be problematic about the communitarian prism. First, and most important, why should we necessarily believe that our community norms reflect the proper moral perspective? Plenty of communities throughout history, from ancient Greece to 20th-century America, have had plenty of norms that are positively reprehensible. The communitarian perspective seems, therefore, to offer an overly relativistic perspective on morality; tolerance can devolve to "anything goes." If morality is defined by a community, how can we judge the obviously flawed morality of a community of racists, for example?

And second, even if our community norms are acceptable, who's to say that we'll be sufficiently guilty or ashamed of violating them? Maybe I just don't care what other people think. And if I'm the sort of person who regularly does awful things, then it's even more likely that I don't. So wondering how I'd feel if everyone in my community knew what I was doing would be unlikely to stop me from doing them.

Here again, then, we can see that we're better positioned to make sophisticated moral choices by using one or more of the other perspectives in conjunction with the communitarian moral prism.

The Utilitarian Prism

"What course(s) of action will best maximize total happiness in the world?"

My friend Johnny was dying. In spite of his illness, though, he remained in good spirits. His sense of humor was as lively as ever, and he never missed an opportunity to make jokes about himself, his visitors, or the incredibly ironic and absurd nature of life in general.

He was having trouble eating; he hadn't much of an appetite and there weren't many foods he could keep down. In fact, during his final few months, he subsisted mainly on bottled water and Triscuit crackers. But in his own inimitable style, he turned this into a production: he created a shrine to the sacred Triscuit and developed an entire quasi-religion to honor them. Every time he finished a box, he'd pile it onto the Great Pyramid of Triscuit that was growing next to his bed. He'd often make light of his fetish for Triscuits and even joked that he'd like his coffin to be constructed out of tasty wheat snacks instead of wood.

I was living in Santa Fe, New Mexico, and was planning a visit out to L.A. to see him one last time. Shopping for a gift to bring him, I spied the perfect thing. In a cooking supply store, affixed to a mini-refrigerator, were half a dozen Triscuit magnets! Fashioned out of rubber, with the fanatic attention to detail one sees in the displays of fake food in the windows of Sushi restaurants, they were perfect replicas of the Nabisco™ snack cracker. I knew Johnny would go crazy over them. I just had to have one for him.

I peeled one off the refrigerator and brought it up to the check-out counter, beaming. "How much?" I asked the owner holding out the fake Triscuit for her to see.

"Those are not for sale," she said, removing it from my hand.

"You're kidding."

"Sorry. I had to go all the way to Japan to get those and they are simply not for sale."

"But you have six of them," I complained. "Just one? What's the difference?"

"Not for sale."

I tried to tell her the story of why I was buying it—how ill my friend Johnny was, how much Triscuits meant to him, and how happy he would be to get it—but she didn't budge. I offered her fifty bucks for it but still no dice. She said there were plenty of other beautiful gift items in the store and I was welcome to look around all I wanted, but the Triscuits, unfortunately, were not for sale.

At this point, I did a little utilitarian calculus. I reckoned how happy Johnny would be to receive the magnet as well as how pleased I would be to give it to him, and compared it to the pain the store owner would experience to be out one of her six magnets, along with the guilt I would feel to have gotten it without paying. The result was obvious. The right thing to do according to the utilitarian moral prism was to steal one of the magnets. So that's what I did. I waited until the owner was out of sight and when she wasn't looking, I slipped one of Triscuits into my pocket. Then, after browsing a suitable amount of time to allay suspicion, I strolled from the store with my purloined magnet hot in hand.

Johnny, of course, was thrilled to receive it. And he was delighted that I stole it. That made it even more precious, more deserving of inclusion in the Triscuit shrine. He stuck the magnet to his bedside lamp where he could see it first thing in the morning and last thing at night. It gave him great pleasure to look at it and be reminded of how strange and wonderful the world and all the people in it are and how he had friends who loved him and who were willing to take risks for him to show that love.

I don't know what happened to the magnet after Johnny died a few months later. I like to think that someone slipped it into the pocket of the suit he was buried in and that it remains with him now in his final resting place, a small testimony to my undying affection for my departed friend.

That the utilitarian moral prism would cause us to judge that I did the right thing by stealing the Triscuit reveals both its strengths and its weaknesses.

On the plus side, it makes good sense to appreciate the critical importance of people's happiness when choosing the right thing to do. A morality that ignores people's feelings runs counter to the way we usually move through the world. The utilitarian perspective recognizes that, in general, we are motivated to seek pleasure and avoid pain, and it builds its perspective on that foundation. Moreover, most of us tend to be natural utilitarians; it's the way we approach not only moral issues but practical matters as well. In this sense, the utilitarian perspective is quite common-sensical; it's not nearly as esoteric as some of the other points of view. And its central principle is quite straightforward. What could be less complicated than "Maximize total happiness"?

On the minus side, utilitarianism is infamous for seeming to let the "ends justify the means," no matter what those means are. If maximizing happiness is all that matters, then it seems that injustices can be committed in the name of making people happy. So, for instance, if it would maximize total happiness to roast national politicians over an open fire (and perhaps it might), we ought to do it. But, of course, that's not right, so utilitarianism is flawed. Moreover, utilitarianism can be unfair to minority viewpoints. Since what is trying to be maximized is *overall* happiness, the pain of someone who falls outside the mainstream can be minimized, if not ignored altogether. Finally, the utilitarian principle, though simply stated, is hard to satisfy. It's easy enough to understand the rule, "maximize happiness," but it's extremely difficult to figure out what particular actions would have that effect.

For all these reasons, we are likely to make better, more sophisticated moral judgments if we temper the utilitarian moral prism with one or more of the others.

The Virtue Ethics Prism

"What would the most virtuous person I know of do in this situation?"

Liz Raibil, a philosopher I know, was teaching an evening course in Introductory Ethics at a community college in the midwest. One night, about halfway through the class, a young man entered the classroom in a state of high agitation. He brandished a revolver and ordered everyone to leave except one woman. She was his estranged girlfriend and he "just wanted to talk to her."

Liz quickly shepherded all her students out the door. But when it was her turn to follow, she paused: should she really leave her student alone in the room with a gun-toting ex-boyfriend? Even if she rushed immediately to alert security, it might be too late to prevent a tragedy. On the other hand, if she stayed, who knows what sort of danger she would be in. And didn't she have some responsibility to the students she'd just evacuated?

Ultimately, she stayed and—in part by her willingness to bear witness—managed to convince the man to put away his gun and surrender to the authorities.

When I heard through the grapevine about what Liz had done, I was amazed. How had she had the heart to stand up for her student in such a potentially explosive situation? How was she able to steel herself, set aside her justifiable fears, and behave in a way that so clearly demonstrated the moral virtue of courage?

I saw her a few weeks later at a philosophy colloquium and asked her how she did it. She told me that she had put a single question to herself: "what would my great-aunt Elsie do in this situation?" Elsie was an 83-year old former schoolteacher who lived in Northern Minnesota on a farm she had run herself since her husband died some thirty years earlier. In her career as an educator and a farmer, she had stood her ground against, among others, religious groups, irate parents, land developers, snowmobilers, and county tax assessors, and her fearlessness, Liz said, was an inspiration. She couldn't imagine that Elsie would have allowed one of her own students to be left alone under life-threatening circumstances.

"I pretended I was Elsie," said Liz. "And I almost felt myself becoming her. Suddenly, I seemed to be seeing the guy with the gun as Elsie would see him—a confused little boy. And he no longer appeared so dangerous as he did sad and lost. I was still scared, but I felt pretty confident that in acting as Elsie would act, I was doing the right thing. At least I was sure that I'd be able to look back on what I did without regret."

Liz was lucky on two counts: first, that everything worked out all right, and second, that she had someone in her life like great-aunt Elsie to appeal to as an ideal. This suggests some of both the strengths and weaknesses of the virtue ethics prism.

Perhaps its greatest asset is that it provides for a straightforward, real-world approach to solving moral problems. We just have to think of our virtuous ideal and imagine what he or she would do in our shoes. But the weakness of this is twofold. First, we may not know someone whose moral judgment we invariably respect, especially in situations that we ourselves find particularly troubling. And second, even if we do, it's not at all clear that we can accurately predict how this person would act. Since virtue ethics doesn't provide a principle to which we can appeal in determining how we ought to act, we're left guessing about the choices someone else would make.

Added to this is the potentially troubling way in which the virtue ethics perspective tends to downplay the consequences of one's choices. In Liz's case, we can unproblematically celebrate her courage because no one got hurt. But suppose the man had shot her for staying? The virtue ethics prism doesn't give us the where-withal to criticize her decision. As long as a person behaves as a virtuous person would, then it doesn't really matter if things turn out badly. Consequently, as with any of the seven perspectives, we are apt to make more sophisticated choices by using the virtue ethics prism in conjunction with one or more of the others.

The Egoistic Prism

"What course(s) of action will most effectively ensure that my short- and long-term goals are reached?"

My tenth wedding anniversary was four days away. Unfortunately, it was an incredibly busy time for me in my work. I had several deadlines all crashing together simultaneously and was scheduled to go out of town for an important meeting the following week. Although I dearly wanted to do something special to celebrate the occasion, I felt overwhelmed and nervous about the prospect. I was far too preoccupied by work-related stresses to imagine what my wife, Jennifer, and I could possibly do to mark the event. The very thought of even taking an evening off filled me with a kind of dread; if I lost a whole night of work, I'd never finish what I had to on schedule.

At the same time, though, I felt incredibly beholden to Jennifer. I knew how important it was to her that we not let the occasion slip away. Rituals are a big deal to her; if there was one thing I had learned in a decade of marriage, it was that I needed to be especially sensitive to important events. More than once I had failed to realize how much a birthday or a holiday meant to her and had, as a consequence, hurt her feelings. So I felt that it was my duty not to blow off our anniversary. But I didn't know how I could give it the attention it deserved; I just didn't have the time to do it right.

Unbeknownst to me, Jennifer was going through pretty much the same thing. She had several grant-application deadlines coming up and was also behind schedule on a sculpture that was due for an exhibition in less than a month. Even though she had big plans for our big day, putting them into action seemed beyond her reach.

The day arrived and we still hadn't agreed on what we were going to do. At breakfast that morning, I tentatively broached the subject. Jennifer's slightly evasive answer made me even more worried that I was dropping the ball. So I took a chance and admitted to her that what I really wanted to do today was to work on my projects. I knew it was our anniversary, but I was just feeling so swamped that the best way for me to celebrate it would be to use the time we would normally spend going out to get caught up. Then we could celebrate the occasion right at some other time.

Silence. My heart dropped through my chest and went thudding across the floor. Jennifer sighed and looked away.

I was just about to say that I was kidding when she turned to me. "You know what?" she said. "I'm feeling the same way. This is just not the day. I need to make some progress on my sculpture, and if I could just get a good long stretch in the studio, I'd feel a lot better about it. So why don't we each take care of our business today, and we'll celebrate our anniversary when you get back from your trip?"

I was floored. A huge weight was lifted from my shoulders. Jennifer and I embraced and set about clearing the breakfast dishes so we could each go off to work. We set a date for our anniversary a couple weeks in the future. And when it came around, we celebrated.

The right thing to do in this situation emerged when each of us decided to pursue our self-interested goals. Before that, when we were both trying to predict and meet the other person's needs, confusion, discomfort, and even a measure of resentment were the result. But when we finally agreed to practice what the novelist and unabashedly egoistic philosopher Ayn Rand calls "the virtue of selfishness," things turned out fine. As a matter of fact, we could have both spared ourselves some real heartache if only we had copped to what we truly wanted in the first place.

We can see here the obvious strength of the egoistic moral prism: the right thing to do will generally accord with what we want. Since what's morally appropriate is determined to be actions that are legitimately within our rational self-interest, we won't experience a tension between what we want to do and what we ought to do. As long as we can figure out what we really want and how best to go about getting it, we can be sure we're doing the right thing.

Of course, the weakness here is equally obvious. Self-interest hardly strikes us as the right touchstone for morality. The selfish choice often seems inimical to the right choice. Doing the right thing is famously *all about* putting one's own interests aside; charity, generosity, and altruism are moral virtues we hold in the highest esteem.

A dyed-in-the-wool egoist will respond that those virtues are perfectly in keeping with self-interest. Being charitable, generous, and altruistic are good for us; in the long run, they help us get what we want by making others admire and trust us more. In fact, the egoist will say, people who claim they're altruists are kidding themselves. If they really did some soul-searching, they'd realize that their motivation was ultimately selfish.

But this response seems to run headlong into the main problem that egoism faces: the egoist's motivation seems questionable. Even if people do the right thing, if the only reason they're doing it is to get something they want, are they *truly* behaving morally? Should we really praise the behavior of the rich industrialist who gives to charity so his company can get tax breaks? Or the actions of a "hero" who captures an escaped criminal just to get the reward? Because of this, egoism alone may not present the most solid foundation for determining the right thing to do. And as with the other perspectives, we may be more apt to make wise moral choices if we use the egoistic prism in conjunction with one or more of the others.

Blending the Spectrum

As we've seen, there are a number of different ways of determining the right thing to do, all of which have unique strengths and weaknesses.

And while each of these approaches intends to provide an answer that any reasonable person would accept, disagreements often arise. This happens, in part, when advocates for one perspective over another focus solely on the judgment that their particular prism makes visible. Here, people are disagreeing *not* because of the underlying moral issue, but rather because they do not share a common perspective on how to determine what's right. And in these cases, becoming aware of the prism that each party is using can help to resolve existing conflicts.

Consider, for example, a disagreement over the morality of paying bribes to foreign officials. Someone applying a utilitarian moral prism might say that doing so is morally acceptable because, after all, societal happiness is maximized if bribes are paid. Conversely, someone applying a virtue ethics moral prism might say that doing so is wrong because a virtuous person wouldn't pay bribes. The disagreement here centers around a difference in focus along the Individual vs. Societal Considerations spectrum: the utilitarian prism is concerned about societal benefits; the virtue ethics prism is concerned with individual improvement. On the other hand, if we recall the Feelings vs. Principles spectrum, we'll note that *both* prisms care about feelings, so it may be possible, in the attempt to find common ground, to start with a discussion of the emotional response to paying bribes. It may be the case that the utilitarian prism will reconsider its definition of happiness. Or the virtue ethics prism may review its consideration of the feelings involved. Similarly, since both prisms focus more on motives than outcomes, a discussion of the consequences of paying bribes may be a place to begin discussion.

It's easy enough to see where there is common ground between each of the seven prisms:

- Between prisms that focus more on *societal considerations* than *individual considerations* (utilitarianism and communitarianism), consider the effects upon society. Ask, "How does this judgment reflect on the society we hope to create and live in?"

- Between prisms that focus more on *individual considerations* than *societal considerations* (ethic of caring, deontology, virtue ethics, egoism, and existentialism), consider effects upon the *individual*. Ask, "What sort of person will result from making this type of judgment/choice?"

- Between prisms more focused on *principles* than *feelings* (deontology, utilitarianism, and egoism), consider the underlying determinant of right and wrong. Ask, "Is there a principle we can apply here that both of us can agree to?"

- Between prisms more focused on *feelings* than *principles* (ethics of caring, virtue ethics, communitarianism, and existentialism), consider the underlying emotional states of the people involved. Ask, "Why do these people feel the way they do about the issue under consideration?"

- Between prisms more focused on *motives* than *outcomes* (deontology, communitarianism, existentialism, and virtue ethics), consider what the people involved hope to accomplish through their judgments. Ask, "What are the goals that those involved in these judgments are trying to reach?"

- Between prisms more focused on *outcomes* than *motives* (ethic of caring, egoism, and utilitarianism), consider the overall effects on the choices that people are considering. Ask, "What will happen to all of us if these judgments are passed?"

Consider some possible moral conflicts:

- An offer of undocumented raw materials from a supplier.

- Lying about a sick day to take your child to the beach.

- You've acquired some inside information about a competitor from a supposedly confidential source; how do you use it?

- A good customer is especially rude to you; what do you do?

- You and your colleague are vying for the same position, and you are given some useful information that you would normally share with him; do you?

- You have some information about upcoming layoffs, and your co-workers ask you about it; do you tell the truth?

How would each of the seven perspectives likely judge these? Consider the first one. Perhaps the communitarian would say that since there is no law against taking undocumented materials, there's nothing wrong with doing so. A utilitarian might say that it would please both parties, so why not? An existentialist might see accepting the materials as an expression of human freedom and so would advocate it. An egoist would have no trouble justifying it, as long as both parties benefited. On the other hand, a deontologist might object on the grounds that if everyone accepted undocumented materials, businesses would suffer. The virtue ethicist might say that it's wrong because virtuous people don't do that sort of thing. And someone using the ethic of caring prism might say that accepting the materials would damage the caring relationship between both parties, so it ought not to be done.

With all these different perspectives, how could we work toward a mutually satisfactory resolution? Here are some examples.

The communitarian and existentialist might find common

ground by discussing the big picture: Would they be satisfied with the societal implications of such a choice? The communitarian perspective might reconsider whether there *ought* to be a law prohibiting such transactions; conversely, the existentialist might be able to temper its perspective by considering what would happen to the freedom of people other than the parties involved. Would the liberty of competitors who weren't similarly advantaged be constrained? This isn't to say that agreement *would* be reached, only that a strategy for accommodation is possible.

Likewise, in the apparent impasse between the utilitarian and virtue ethics perspectives, common ground might be approached by considering the end picture: Would they both be satisfied with the individual and societal results of such a choice? The utilitarian perspective might reconsider whether—in light of the sort of person one becomes by overlooking regulations—overall happiness really would result; conversely, the virtue ethics perspective might compromise by examining more carefully what the effects of such behavior on a person's character would *really* be given the particulars of the situation at hand.

Or, the ethic of caring perspective might achieve a compromise with the egoist by imagining how the individuals involved would be affected. What would happen to the emotional state of both persons? The egoist might reconsider whether, taking into account the guilt that the customer and vendor might feel, it really was in his or her best interest to take part in such a shady transaction. The ethic of caring perspective might wonder whether the feelings of care that each person had for the other would indeed be nurtured by allowing the deal to take place. Again, doing so wouldn't guarantee that a compromise would be reached, but thinking in these terms could provide a forum for further discussion.

Here we see how apparently intractable moral disagreements can at least be explored—if not solved—by different perspectives on the issues. The lesson is not that *all* such disagreements are resolvable, but only that, by expanding the moral spectrum, we can discover potential ways to work toward common ground. We can recognize that it may indeed be possible to reach mutually accept-able but previously unseen solutions.

When we're able to resolve moral conflicts peacefully and pro-ductively, our personal and professional lives are improved. One might even say the world is made a little bit better place. And it all begins with broadening our moral perspective. This is how we im-prove our ability to perceive and choose the right thing to do.

Expanding the Palette

Each of us can improve our ability to perceive and choose the right thing to do by expanding our own moral spectrum. By drawing each of the seven perspectives into our own and coming to conclu-sions from the standpoint of, not just one, but seven different ways of looking at the issue, we naturally arrive at choices that are more likely to reflect our deepest, most abiding values.

Of course, it's easier said than done. But not impossible. Consider the experience of my friends Bev and Brian, who were having a lot of problems with their 17-year-old daughter, Kelly.

Kelly has never been a particularly studious sort of girl; she's been always much more interested in hanging out with her friends and exploring the great outdoors than in reading or doing school-work. She's a good kid, though, with a great sense of humor and a sensitivity to others that seems pretty rare, especially in younger people. But around the time she turned 16, Kelly really started act-ing out. Maybe it's partly because her parents didn't always have a lot of time to spend with her—both Bev and Brian have full-time careers. Maybe it's partly because she has no strong sense of com-munity—Brian's job as a sales manager for a growing high-tech company has led them to move to three new cities in the past seven years. Or maybe it was just the teenage hormones kicking in. In any case, almost overnight, Kelly went from being your typical moody teenager to an unusually disturbed adolescent. She started hanging out with a different crowd of kids, some of whom suppos-edly had affiliations with street gangs in the L.A. suburb where Bev and Brian lived. She started cutting school regularly, sometimes taking off for two or three days in a row. She apparently began experimenting with drugs; Bev and Brian, nonsmokers, could easily detect the telltale odor of marijuana on her clothes when she came home. But worst of all for them, who, as children of the 70s, had fully expected that some recreational substance use would be part of their daughter's adolescent challenges, was that Kelly was arrested for driving while intoxicated.

When they brought Kelly home that night and failed miserably in trying to engage her in a discussion about the unacceptability of her behavior, Bev and Brian knew something had to be done, but they didn't know what. Should they enroll Kelly in a residential treatment program of some type? Should they investigate boarding schools? Should they quit their jobs and devote themselves full-time to their daughter's care? Should they just look the other way and pretend nothing was happening? Bev and Brian were convinced that there had to be a right answer—an answer that worked best for Kelly and them—but they felt overwhelmed at the possibility of finding it.

I talked to them about the moral spectrum model. Bev and Brian realized that their typical perspective on such issues was best represented by the deontological prism. They usually kept in mind a principle—something like, "Kids have a duty to obey their parents"—and how failing to follow this principle would affect someone: "Well, if they don't, that is, if Kelly doesn't, she'll turn into an obnoxious, disrespectful, and unruly person." On the basis of this perspective, Bev and Brian were leaning in favor of having their daughter packed off to a boarding school of some kind, some place that would really teach Kelly to take responsibility for her behavior. They knew that all three of them would be unhappy if this happened, but it seemed to them the right thing to do.

They began by considering what an ethic of caring perspective would say. No particular answer leapt out; however, it made it clear that *whatever* the right thing to do was, it would allow Kelly to see how deeply Bev and Brian cared for her. Any sort of "tough love" choice would need to emphasize love over toughness.

Taking the utilitarian perspective, the parents could see that a choice that would make them all miserable could never be considered the preferred choice. While this alone wasn't enough to sway them, it did help them continue exploring other options. "I'm sure it would be most painless if we just ignored things," said Bev, "but that doesn't seem right to me either."

Nevertheless, taking into account the utilitarian perspective did convince them to go a little easier on Kelly and themselves. "I've got to learn to pick my battles," Brian said. "Not everything has to turn into a contest of wills. I know she's going to do things that I disagree with. But if they're basically harmless and if they make her happy, why should I complain?"

How could the communitarian perspective inform Bev and Brian's decision? Trusting their natural feelings of sympathy and compassion, they were both inclined to quit their jobs and devote full-time care to Kelly. But keeping in mind the societal implications of that choice put the brakes on it. They figured a communitarian would ultimately say that we should appeal to the institutions that we, as a society, have developed to rear difficult children in the most loving way possible. This inspired them to explore counseling resources that they hadn't previously investigated.

Taking the virtue ethics perspective made Bev and Brian curious to find out what people they admired would say. They talked to their daughter's high school principal, a woman whose judgment they had both long respected. They also got in touch with their family physician, a man who always seemed to them to be the embodiment of a virtuous person. They even solicited the opinion of one of Kelly's childhood friends, a girl named Sarah, from whom Kelly had drifted some but whom Bev thought was one of most level-headed kids she'd ever known.

The existentialist prism seemed at first to say they ought to just let Kelly do her own thing. Her freedom would be maximized if she were allowed to explore her own choices; and Bev and Brian would have the liberty to carry on with their lives, as well. But on closer examination, it became clear that Kelly's long-term freedoms would be compromised if she continued behaving in the way she was. If she didn't start applying herself more in high school, she wouldn't have many options to attend college and her life's prospects would be constrained. So it was obvious that getting Kelly back on track with her education was a priority; otherwise, she would be facing many closed doors in the future.

Finally, the egoistic perspective made Bev and Brian aware of the urgency of doing something. Every day that the issue wasn't resolved was a day in which their own interests—and Kelly's, too—were being thwarted. Whatever decision they came to, therefore, had to be done as quickly as possible.

Nevertheless, combining all the perspectives and coming to a final decision on what to do wasn't something that happened overnight. Bev and Brian took weeks going back and forth over the various ways of looking at the problem. And in the end, it wasn't as if one of them won out. When all was said and done, they ended up opting for a variety of steps inspired by the different approaches. Bev cut back on some of her hours at work to spend more time with Kelly. They made a commitment to joint counseling; the family agreed to meet once a week with a psychologist to discuss what was going on with them. They arranged to have Kelly transferred into a special program in her school district for kids with disciplinary problems; they attend an alternative "school within a school" that's both less and more structured; their curriculum is more free-form, but the requirements for attendance and participation are stricter. Finally, they tried to help Kelly find some sort of mentor in her life. This wasn't easy, since Kelly was singularly uninterested in what any of her parents' adult acquaintances had to say about life. Bev was, however, successful in encouraging Kelly to reestablish a relationship with her old friend Sarah, whose influence, Bev thought, seemed to be pretty positive.

From Bev and Brian's example, you can see the value of expanding the moral spectrum. It may not necessarily yield the one and only one right answer. Sometimes the process will reveal previously unrecognized possibilities. For my friends, the right thing to do was a combination of options. Pursuing all of these represented the right strategy for them to take. It involved a kind of balancing act. They held in their minds each of the seven perspectives and examined the implications. Although they weren't contradictory, they did suggest different courses of action. Bev and Brian were, however, able to draw upon the combined intelligence of these possibilities to see which ones were right for them.

In many ways, Bev and Brian's experience is typical of how the moral spectrum approach works. Key to it is the generation and exploration of options. From this, it may sometimes happen that the one right answer will emerge. In such a case, it will be the combined perspectives of all seven moral spectra that provides our direction. But this sort of result is more typical when we're facing a relatively simple "yes" or "no" type question.

Imagine that you're trying to decide whether to fudge on your income taxes about your home office expenses. You might reason as follows. Existentialism would indicate you should fudge: having the extra few dollars would allow you liberties you otherwise wouldn't have. The deontological prism would recommend against fudging: imagine a world in which everyone adopted your willingness to cheat: The effects on society would be disastrous; you wouldn't want to live in such a world. The ethic of caring prism also would say don't cheat; to do so would be to undermine the caring relationship between you and your fellow citizens. Examining the issue through the communitarian prism would indicate you ought not to fudge; if everyone in your community knew what you were up to, you wouldn't do it. The utilitarian prism would indicate you ought to: the relatively large amount of happiness that you will gain outweighs the relatively small amount of unhappiness of cheated-upon government officials—who aren't likely to find out anyway. The virtue ethics prism would say it's wrong since the most virtuous person you know wouldn't do what you're considering. Finally, egoism unproblematically would say "go for it." So, in this case, by a 4 to 3 vote, not fudging wins out.

More often as not, though, several possibilities will come to the fore. Choosing among them may be a matter, as it was for Bev and Brian, of trying things out and seeing what works. Or it may be a process of elimination that results in one or more choices taking precedence. In any case, the benefits of having a rich array of possible options makes the approach extremely useful when faced not only with moral choices but with choices of all types. The likelihood of arriving at decisions that truly are reflective of our dearest and deepest values increases as the sophistication of our available alternatives goes up.

The moral spectrum approach thus does not always immediately yield the easy and obvious answer. Sometimes it is part of a process that moves us incrementally closer to where we need to go. But this in itself is real progress—and often just the push we need to eventually discover the right answer. And this is the case, as we will see in the chapter to come, not only in our personal lives but in business and professional experiences as well.

Chapter Three

Right at Work

Doing Right by Co-workers and Customers

Business Ethics: An Oxymoron?

Most businesspeople are interested in doing the right thing—up to a point. Most of us, on the job, adhere to a code of business ethics. But this code is usually pretty businesslike; we might reasonably question whether it's ethical. When the dual demands of conscience and competition pull us in conflicting directions, competition often wins out. We justify our behavior by telling ourselves that everyone does it. Or that business is a special game with different rules for what's acceptable. No doubt both of these responses are true. But what does that say about our code of business ethics? And what does it imply for the moral legacy we are leaving?

In a perfect world, we'd never have to ask whether something was good or just good for business. In a perfect world, there would be a direct correspondence between people's character and their success on the job. In a perfect world, there would be no rich slumlords, no sleazy but successful salespeople, no cruel and heartless corporate leaders. The perfect world would be a corporate world of instant karma: as soon as somebody did something underhanded, ruthlessly competitive, or downright illegal, his or her business would suffer. Organizations that refused to do the right thing would fail miserably; individuals who treated co-workers and customers unjustly would quickly find themselves out on the street.

But, unfortunately, we don't live in a perfect world. It's perfectly obvious that good things do happen to bad businesspeople: and that there are plenty of not-so-nice businesspeople out there.

The news is filled with stories of embezzlement and fraud. We regularly read about businesspeople skirting corporate policies and industry regulations to line their own pockets will ill-gotten gains. Reports abound of companies, too, that make shady deals to maximize profit at the expense of their employees, their customers, and the environment.

The public sector is no better than the world of private enterprise. The Washington state auditor, for instance, recently reported that state employees swiped over $1.5 million dollars a year from state agencies and local governments for their personal use. The schemes ranged from complex forgeries using optical scanners and color computer printers to simple tricks such as stealing highway signs and selling them for scrap metal.

And these are only the people who get caught! Equally bad—or far worse—behavior goes on all the time right under our unsuspecting noses. All around us, businesspeople—from the corner deli vendor who sells a three-ounce "quarter pounder" to the multinational CEO whose salary is 100 times greater than her company's average wage-earner—are doing morally objectionable things and getting away with it. In fact, the ability to not get caught has essentially become the litmus test for what's acceptable in business: as long as nobody blows the whistle on you, whatever you're doing counts as okay.

Ironically, though, businesspeople are by and large interested in ethical issues and are genuinely concerned about doing the right thing in regard to their co-workers, customers, and suppliers. In a small survey I conducted of some thirty organizations in the Seattle area, nearly all of my respondents reported that they had systems, training, and personnel in place for helping managers and employees to make good choices. For the most part, companies want to be good corporate citizens. And the people who work there want to be considered morally upstanding as well. It's not as if employees check their consciences at the front gate. While the temptation for both individuals and organizations to lie, cheat, and swindle may be there all the time, it's clear that not everyone always succumbs to them.

Moreover, increasingly, businesses *do* make a connection between doing good and doing well. Companies like mail-order marketer Smith & Hawken and recycled carpet manufacturer Interface, Inc., are well-known for adhering to the highest standards of ethical behavior—and they attribute their success directly to doing so.

Within organizations, "ethical leadership" has become more than just a buzzword, as executives recognize that employees perform better when they are treated in accordance with principles of justice, fairness, and, as Kant would put it, as "ends" rather than simply a means to maximizing profit or increasing efficiency. Co-workers, too, in their interactions with one another, are generally quite committed to following some variation of a moral principle like the Golden Rule. Colleagues make an effort to treat colleagues as they themselves would like to be treated—not just because it affords them the best chance of being treated in a like manner, but because it's the right thing to do.

So with all this interest in doing the right thing, how come so many organizations and individuals fail to meet their very own standards? Why do we continue to see endless reports of people and the companies they work for engaging in behavior that is objectionable, if not downright reprehensible?

You might argue that it's just ignorance. If people knew better what the right thing to do was, then they'd have no problem doing it. You might even interpret that as the message of this book, which seems to be suggesting that a good deal of the reason we aren't as successful at making the right choice is that we can't determine what it is.

But this would be to tie morality a bit too closely to knowledge. It would be to say that the only reason we ever fail to do the right thing is a lack of information or understanding. And while this is a refreshingly optimistic view of human nature, it's hardly realistic. Lots of perfectly vile actions are done by people who know exactly what they're doing. Plus, it's obvious that we regard people who are misinformed differently than people who willingly do bad things. Ignorance is no excuse, but it's usually a mitigating factor. Compare how you'd judge a car dealer who intentionally sold you a lemon compared to one who wasn't aware that the vehicle had problems.

It would seem, then, that doing the right thing is more than just a matter of knowing what it is—and also that knowing the right thing is more than just having a dry collection of facts. Especially at work, where the demands of self-interest and morality tug at us in opposing ways, it's incumbent upon each of us to broaden our moral perspective so the choices we make are aligned with our deepest values. In this way, the work that we do and the way we do it becomes an authentic expression of who we are and what we believe in.

The implicit assumption here, though, is that it makes sense to be a good person or, more specifically, that it makes good business sense to be a good businessperson. And of course, this is quite contentious: the common wisdom is that "nice guys finish last." But do they? Or are they just running a different race?

Do Nice Guys Really Finish Last?

Philosophers are always trying to "reconcile" self-interest and morality. In business terms, they are attempting to make good deeds pay off in good results; they are trying to make sure that doing well goes hand-in-hand with doing good. Unfortunately, their efforts tend to be less than convincing for a number of reasons.

First, even if self-interest points us in the same direction as morality most of the time, there will still be plenty of occasions when we have an incentive to act immorally in service of our own selfish ends. Imagine for instance that you're having an important sales meeting with a prospective client. During the meeting, she gets called from the room, says she'll be back in five minutes, and asks you just to sit tight. After she's gone, you notice a proposal from your biggest competitor sitting half-opened on her desk. No one will ever know if you quickly glance at their bid. Self-interest tells you that you'd be a fool not to look; morality says that to do so would be wrong, even though the benefits of doing so are great. So what do you do? Clearly there's a tension between what's right and what's prudent; morality and self-interest are not so easily reconciled.

Suppose, though, you decide that self-interest dictates that you ought not to look. Maybe the situation is a set-up: your client left the room just to test whether or not you're trustworthy; even now, she's hiding behind a one-way mirror watching to see what you'll do. So you don't turn your competitor's bid over, but the reason you don't is a selfish one, not a moral one. If so, this illustrates another reason philosophers find it difficult to reconcile self-interest with morality—if our motivation is purely self-interested, then it hardly seems that our actions count as moral. Doing the right thing for the wrong reasons isn't really doing the right thing.

But the main explanation for why "reconcilers" fail isn't nearly so theoretical. Rather, it's the simple matter of empirical evidence. Observation seems to indicate that it often doesn't make sense to do the right thing. Good people aren't as successful as bad people. Only suckers follow the rules. The right thing to do can't possibly be the self-interested thing to do because "nice guys finish last."

But let us ask again: *Do they really?*

Consider the businessperson who, for me, is the paradigm of a nice guy: my father-in-law, Bob Dixon. Bob spent most of his career in the oil business, an industry not particularly known for adhering to the highest standards of ethical behavior. Bob, by contrast, always conducted his affairs with utmost regard for customers and co-workers and in the strictest accordance to federal regulations, local ordinances, and principles of fair play. As chief financial officer for a successful regional oil refining and distributing company, he had plenty of opportunities for playing fast and loose with things, but he never did. Every time a choice presented itself between the right thing to do and the expedient-but-morally questionable thing to do, he chose the former—even if it meant passing up a short-term chance to make a quick buck for either the company or himself.

In the mid-1970s, dissatisfied with the performance and direction of the company, Bob put together a bid to purchase it from its owner, a man with whom—on both business and personal matters—he didn't always see eye-to-eye.

Sometime during the negotiations, Bob got visited by an official from the Environmental Protection Agency. It had come to the attention of the EPA that one of the company's storage tanks was "hot"; that is, it was filled with leaded gasoline, not unleaded, as had been reported. The significance of this was twofold.

First, it meant that the company's owner had illegally sold some of its federally issued "lead credits." (At that time, oil refiners were issued such credits by the EPA to limit their production of leaded gas, which was cheaper to refine but worse for air quality. Companies that produced less leaded gas than their allotment of credits permitted were allowed to sell leftover credits on the open market to companies that had produced more leaded gas than they had credits for.) Since the gas in the tank was leaded, the credits ought to have been applied to its production and ought not to have been available to sell. However, because the existence of the gas became known only when it was sold, an unscrupulous businessperson could put the leaded product in a holding tank and no one would be the wiser. This meant he made money both coming and going—once, by being able to less expensively produce the leaded gas, and twice, by illegally selling the credits.

Second, the existence of the so-called "hot tank" meant that the owner was planning to skirt EPA regulations by eventually mixing the leaded gas back into unleaded, thus enabling him to cover his tracks. Obviously, though, this led to more lead being released into the atmosphere, which was precisely what the regulations were intended to prevent.

The EPA had come to investigate Bob because they figured he must be in on the scam. They reasoned that Bob, as prospective owner of the company, had to know about the "hot tank" and was probably planning to profit from it the same way his predecessor had. In fact, Bob was completely unaware of the current president's shady dealings. But he had no proof. And to make matters worse, the current president was claiming that *he* was the one who was ignorant; Bob was actually trying to purchase the company to cover *his* tracks.

Facing stiff fines and a potential jail term, Bob had nothing to protect him but his reputation. But as it turned out, that was enough. Colleagues, customers, and competitors alike vouched for his character. Everyone the EPA talked to insisted that Bob couldn't possibly be behind the "hot tank" scheme. Such behavior would be entirely inconsistent with the man they knew, a man who literally embodied virtue in his personal and professional relations.

The EPA had no choice but to lay off. Instead, they went after the company controller, a fellow whose reputation was not nearly so stellar as Bob's. Eventually, he too was exonerated, but not without spending a lot of money on legal advice and representation.

So here we have a case in which a nice guy didn't finish last. In spite of having to defend himself against far more ruthless associates, he came out on top. The long-term advantage of having a good reputation far outweighed any short-term benefit he might have gained by being more like them.

Of course, there are two common objections to this. First is that the *really* ruthless businessperson will simply fake being nice. After all, if the only reason to play fair is to earn a good reputation, then the prudent thing to do is be nice when others are watching and vicious when they're not. It probably makes sense to treat co-workers well—especially higher-ups—since their perception of you is critical, but vendors and competitors—who don't have much effect on your reputation—can be treated like dirt. Clever businesspeople then, will be those who always get away with as much as possible. With a smile on their face, they are shaking hands with one hand, stabbing you in the back with the other.

The problem with this objection, though, is that it's extremely difficult for someone to successfully mimic the sort of behavior that will earn them a good reputation. We're quite good at detecting phonies; if someone is only pretending to be nice, we usually can sense it. Sure we may get fooled once, even twice, but a reputation is a function of repeated interactions over time. And very few, if any, people are good enough actors and have good enough memories to consistently pull off the trick time after time. As Mark Twain said, "If you tell the truth, you don't have to remember anything." It's far easier to *actually* be honest and forthright than to pretend to be.

Taking this one step further, economist Robert Frank has proposed that evolution itself has ultimately selected for authentically moral behavior. In his lively and refreshingly accessible *Passions Within Reason*, Frank offers a theory that purports to explain why human beings have evolved a system of morality even though it's not obviously in their self-interest to do the right thing. He attempts to show why it sometimes makes sense for people to act in ways that—from a straightforward self-interested perspective—appear to be irrational. Broadly, Frank argues that the single-minded pursuit of self-interest (which "flint-eyed researchers" in the social sciences have long considered the paradigm of rational activity) often prevents people from attaining their preferred ends. Behaving irrationally—that is, being motivated by emotions such as anger, empathy, even love—pays off better in the long run. Having such emotions and being motivated by them enables people to cooperate with others in ways that would otherwise be impossible. So, for instance, despite there being no rational self-interested reason I ought to leave a tip for a waiter in a restaurant to which I'll never return, it still makes sense for me to do so since, by doing so, I will sustain my predisposition to be a "good guy," which, in turn, will allow other people (especially waiters, I guess) to recognize that I am an amiable fellow who regularly keeps his promises (especially to tip well) and who, consequently, ought to be cooperated with—and more to the point, who ought to be brought his martini and appetizers as quickly as possible.

But if we set aside this alleged advantage of being a nice guy, we still have to respond to a second objection: What about the many times when it *does* so happen that doing the right thing means we get screwed? What about all those instances when it really does seem as if the nice guy finishes last?

Consider again Bob Dixon. After the oil industry went bust in the 1980s, Bob took a job as president of an independent manufacturer of custom motorized wheelchairs. It was a family-owned company with an excellent product but sorely in need of professional leadership. Bob believed in the staff, respected the owner's vision, and recognized the organization's potential to both help people and earn a substantial profit. The job required a great deal of commitment in terms of both time and energy. A lot of travel, some of it international, was involved. To be closer to the production facility, Bob relocated to a part of the country that neither he nor his wife had ever lived in before; they bought a home two thousand miles away from their family and nearly all of their lifelong friends. He even—as a way to improve cash flow and acquire a greater share of operating authority—invested a large sum of his own savings in the company. And for a while, things looked great: orders were up, production efficiency was increasing, morale was high.

But all the while, unbeknownst to Bob, the company's owner had his own devious agenda. Perhaps it was a matter of being psychologically unable to relinquish any measure of real control over the company he had created; perhaps it was simple greed. In any case, he was secretly undercutting Bob's efforts even as he supported them outwardly. Time and again, he failed to carry through his part of agreed-upon marketing efforts. He lied about having made staff cuts and reassignments Bob had recommended. And he secretly spent huge amounts of company revenues on personal projects that he had promised Bob he would discontinue.

Ultimately, the owner's actions—and inactions—destroyed the profitability that Bob's work had initially led to. But the kicker was that the owner blamed Bob for the company's failure and had him terminated by the board of directors. Bob ended up losing not only his job, but a substantial monetary investment.

Friends and family members commiserated with Bob, reminding him that it's a dog-eat-dog world in which lying, cheating, and double-crossing pay big returns. They asked him why he didn't retaliate against the company owner with underhanded dealings of his own. Shouldn't he have stuck it to him somehow, even if it meant compromising his own ethical standards? Didn't he know that nice guys finish last?

Bob said he didn't see it that way. When we talked about the experience, he expressed some remorse over not having seen what was happening, but he had no qualms about having stayed true to his own principles in responding. Never once was he tempted to retaliate by lying, cheating, or double-crossing. I asked how he felt about things, seeing as how he got the serious short end of the stick—even though he was the one who had done all the right things. Did he agree with everyone else that he ought not to have been such a "nice guy"?

Bob said that the important thing was that he still slept well at night. He could get up in the morning and see the man in the mirror and could look him right in the eye. Bob didn't think this was true for his ex-boss; even though he might try to deny it, his moral legacy was one that he would be unable to look back upon proudly. Bob, on the other hand, said his conscience was clear. He made his choices and had no trouble living with them. So, as far as he was concerned, he didn't lose at all. And he wouldn't trade places with his ex-boss for all the money in the world.

I was convinced—and still am. "Nice guys"—men and women who are willing to do the right thing even if self-interest dictates otherwise—gain a priceless reward that is unavailable to liars, cheats, and double-crossers. Bob called it a good night's sleep. We might identify it simply as integrity.

The Business of Integrity

Life- and career-planning expert Dick Leider defines integrity as "keeping the small promises you make to yourself." He means to focus our attention on the choices we make when no one else is around, the choices that define ourselves to ourselves.

A similar idea is explored by philosopher Alisdair MacIntyre, who talks about the critical task of developing a coherent narrative of one's life. For MacIntyre, we can achieve happiness and meaning in our lives only by situating ourselves within a story that makes sense given the person we are trying to be.[6] Integrity, then, will be a matter of holding attitudes and making choices that are consistent with the character of that person. Moreover, since happiness is tied to human flourishing and such flourishing depends on a kind of excellence in thought and action, those attitudes and choices will *necessarily* accord with a good character, one that embodies the best qualities of human beings.

In our business and personal lives, we achieve integrity when we express the things we care about through the things that we do. Another way of putting this is to say that we achieve integrity when our *values* and our *virtues* are in alignment. Values are expressions of our emotions; they're what we desire. Virtues are character

---

[6]MacIntyre, Alisdair, *After Virtue* (Notre Dame: Notre Dame Press, 1984). See discussion around pages 200–205.

traits; they are dispositions to behave in particular ways in order to get or hold onto the things we value. Our values reveal *what* we feel is important; our virtues reveal *how* we feel those values ought to be realized.

For example, many people strongly value a sense of community in both their business and personal lives. They feel that meaningful interpersonal and professional relationships are vital to a life well lived. They might have different opinions, however, about which virtues would best sustain that value. Someone might say that honesty is key; unless people always tell the truth, the community's foundations will be undermined. Someone else might contend that compassion is the more important virtue; "little white lies" are tolerable in the name of greasing the wheels of social interaction. Here they agree on *what* is valuable, but they disagree on *how* to go about valuing it.

In recent years, the practice of "values clarification" has been much discussed and argued about. Basically the simple practice of helping people—usually students—identify the attitudes, behaviors, and goals they care most about, values clarification has been alternately heralded as the foundation of an authentic appreciation for diversity and castigated as the source of contemporary society's decay. Neither of these positions is fair to an activity that in and of itself is fairly benign. Of course it can be quite enlightening for people to get a clearer picture of their value system; but this is hardly the sole basis for positive social change. And yes, there is a danger of collapsing moral distinctions if people merely present their values noncritically; but it would be a gross overstatement to claim that values clarification is therefore responsible for antisocial behavior or lack of respect for authority.

The real problem with values clarification is that it only answers the *what* question—what we feel is important. It fails, however, to connect up to the *how* question—how we feel those values ought to be realized. It allows us to see the things we care most about, but it doesn't help us clarify the character of a person who cares about those things. This makes it difficult to examine our values critically and change them. Values clarification can, for example, help me see that I value truth, justice, and the American Way, but it doesn't enable me to assess whether I really value being the sort of person who holds those values. There's no real room for reflecting on what I think I *ought* to value.

By linking up values and virtues, however, self-examination becomes possible. Virtue, in this context, can be understood as a character trait that supports a particular value or set of values. For example, suppose I value independence. What character traits—fixed dispositions to behave in a certain way—enable me to express that value in the world? Courage and honesty come to mind. In order to be independent, I have to be courageous enough to take a stand on my own and sufficiently honest about my intentions that people will accord me the independence I value. Knowing this, I can then reflect upon whether someone who is courageous and honest is the sort of person I value being. Presumably, it will be.

Compare this to a case in which I highly value monetary success. The virtues necessary to achieving this success might include aggressiveness and competitiveness. Reflecting on this sort of person, I may realize that that's not the sort of character I wish to cultivate. I may then undertake to reassess my value, perhaps even to discard it.

None of this is to guarantee that linking values and virtues solves all the problems associated with values clarification. However, it does seem to address the concern that all values are equally valuable. Moreover, by helping us to ensure that the values we hold are actually the ones we feel we ought to hold, establishing these links can enable us to more consistently choose those actions that reflect what we really do care about. And for businesspeople who are committed to personal integrity in word and deed, this is crucial.

Values and Virtue Clarification

The first step, then, is to do a little values clarification. Consider the following list. Identify which of the following values you hold. Add your own to come up with a number of key values that you hold most dear.

- Security
- Cooperation
- Truth
- Spirituality
- Quiet
- Fun
- Community
- Children
- Technology
- Health
- Relaxation

- Variety
- Power
- Friendship
- Recognition
- Order
- Newness
- Autonomy
- Nature
- Recreation
- Family
- Peace

- Tradition
- Wealth
- Freedom
- Learning
- Change
- Advancement
- Teamwork
- Society
- Work
- Knowledge
- Excitement

Having developed your list, now consider the virtues necessary for expressing those values. Consider the following list of virtues. Add your own to come up with a number of virtues that support the values you hold.

- Competitiveness
- Generosity
- Friendliness
- Artistic skill
- Loyalty
- Confidence
- Speed
- Compassion

- Predictability
- Courage
- Honesty
- Understanding
- Humility
- Cleverness
- Thoughtfulness
- Flexibility

- Perseverance
- Temperance
- Ready wit
- Good judgment
- Creativity
- Thrift
- Fortitude
- Determination

Now, think about the character of the person who embodies the virtues that you have identified. Is this the sort of person you really want to be? Or is there a "disconnect" between *what* you value and *how* you value it? If so, consider which of your values you may not *really* value. See if you can revise your list of values so that things closest to your heart can most appropriately be expressed by the person closest to whom you really are.

Integrity in Business

Getting our values and virtues in alignment can help us achieve a heightened sense of personal integrity. But how does this translate into our professional lives? As businesspeople, we often confront situations that call our integrity into question. Is there anything we can do to ensure that the manner in which we address things represents an appropriate expression of the person we are trying to be?

Consider some of the moral issues that businesspeople typically face on the job. In my discussions with corporate leaders and ethics officers, three main areas of concern tend to come out. They are:

- Conflicts of interest, especially in dealing with customers/clients

- Workplace issues, especially around issues of diversity

- Employee loyalty, non-competition, and technology transfer issues, especially around cases of proprietary information

Let's look at an example of each of these and see if an alignment of values and virtues might help us choose the right thing to do.

Conflicts over Conflicts of Interest

A classic conflict of interest presented itself to my friend Sue Simon, who—in her first job out of journalism school—got hired as editor of a small daily paper in a rural Minnesota town. In the position, she wore many hats: reporter, layout designer, office manager; she even helped deliver papers when the regular guy was sick. The one area in which she had little input was sales; both advertising and subscription contracts were handled by the newspaper's owner's brother George, who had been with the paper for years.

About six months into the job, Sue discovered that Carl Larson, owner of Larson's Hardware, one of the paper's oldest and most important advertisers, had been accused of sexual harassment by a former employee, a college student who worked after school and during the summers as cashier.

To Sue, this was big news. She wanted to run the story on the front page with photos of Larson and his accuser. Readers would want to know all the details of the upcoming trial; Sue saw regular updates, perhaps with input from an expert on legal affairs from the University of Minnesota.

George, however, vehemently disagreed. He said that the story ought to be killed, or at least, relegated to the back page. He'd talked with Carl, who said that the whole thing was a misunderstanding; the girl had gone off to college and gotten a lot of funny ideas in her head. He hadn't done anything wrong and when all the facts came out, there'd be nothing there. In the meantime, Carl hoped that George would see to it that nobody on the paper lost his or her head about it and started printing all sorts of rumor and innuendo. And just so they knew how serious he was, he wanted to let George know that if the paper did cover the story in a big way, he was going to cancel his advertising contracts immediately.

Sue argued that just because Larson's was a big advertiser was no reason not to run the news. It wasn't as if they were making anything up; the accusation and trial were to be a matter of public record. Sure, agreed George, but why did that mean they had to feature it in headlines? Wasn't news about the town's upcoming "Pioneer Homestead Days" celebration a bigger deal, anyway? And besides, without Larson's continued advertising support, the paper might not make it. They were operating at their financial limits already; a setback like this would probably spell their doom.

Obviously, Sue was torn. Her instincts as a journalist told her one thing; her responsibilities as a businessperson told her another. Moreover, she knew Carl Larson; he wasn't a bad guy—kind of old-fashioned and sort of patronizing, but not really a creep. She felt bad about the prospect of reporting on him, but if the accusations held up in court, then he certainly deserved to be exposed.

What should she do? How could she decide? She tried asking herself the seven moral prism questions.

Unfortunately, her answers were inconclusive. She felt that publishing the story would probably lead to less happiness in the universe. However, she was pretty sure that the person she admired most in the world, her college journalism professor, would have run it. On the other hand, she thought that as a model for universal behavior, the decision to publish wasn't the greatest. She wasn't sure she would want to live in a world where truth always triumphed over compassion. But the idea that her journalistic colleagues might find out that she'd killed the story haunted her; she'd be mortified if all her friends knew she'd caved in to pressure from the marketplace. From an egoistic standpoint, it seemed right to publish the story, but the ethic of caring prism suggested that she put her relationship with Carl above journalistic success. Finally, the existentialist perspective was rather confounding. Sue couldn't tell if human freedom was enhanced by her liberty to run the story or Carl's liberty to see it squelched. So it wasn't as if the right thing to do just jumped out at her. Her intuitions, even informed by thoughtful reflection, provided no clear direction as to what she ought to do.

What eventually helped, though, was to think about values and virtues. Sue took some time to identify what her core values were. Nothing was closer to her heart than community, autonomy, and truth. The virtues that supported these values were, for her, primarily understanding and courage. With that in mind, she tried to act in a way that embodied these aspects of character. What came out of that was her decision to publish the story, but do so in a different way. Instead of making it an explicit exposé of Larson's behavior, she put together a feature on sexual harassment in the workplace in which the allegations against Larson were discussed. Her goal was to stand up for her convictions but do so in a way that demonstrated an understanding for the needs of her paper, her community, and for the people involved in the case.

Now, you might say that Sue caved in. Or, you might argue that she was unreasonably inflexible. But neither of these—at least from her perspective—would be quite true. The fact is, she ultimately arrived at a choice that allowed her to act with integrity—an alignment of virtues and values—in a manner consistent with her concern about what the right thing to do was. It may not have been a perfect solution, but it was one she could live with, one that allowed her to keep the small promises she made to herself, and to still get a good night's sleep.

Workplace Issues: Those Who Can't Do, Teach

Like conflicts of interest, workplace issues—especially as they relate to employee diversity—present ethical dilemmas that are often quite difficult to solve. Examples range from simple differences of opinion over what personal items employees ought to have on their desks to complex policy concerns around hiring, training, and promotion. Figuring out what's the right thing to do in such cases is especially difficult because the diverse perspectives of the people involved are often so difficult to reconcile. This inclines people to say that there is no right answer, that what's right for one person is wrong for another and never the twain shall meet.

But this is to overstate the problem. Certainly, there is plenty of room for conflict. And probably, there is more than one way of settling it. But this doesn't mean that *every* solution is as good as every other, nor that by using a process to think about things, better solutions can't be arrived at.

This was made obvious to me in a workplace situation that ironically involved corporate training professionals—a group of people who, you'd think, ought to know better but who, as a matter of fact, need just as much help with these issues as anyone else does.

The organization where this example took place was an exciting start-up company, a bold new venture that was going to change the face not only of our parent company but, we hoped, of the entire human resource and development industry. We often said that "our most important product is not the one we are making but the one we *are*." It was our hope that the 35 or 40 of us were creating a model for how corporations and their employees would work together in the future.

Consequently, we had a lot of meetings: project kick-off meetings, regular update meetings, planning meetings, preplanning meetings. For the most part, they were productive, but from time to time, it did seem as if they got in the way of getting anything done.

When deadlines loomed, it was often difficult to make all these conferences—especially our regularly scheduled 4:00 Friday afternoon staff meeting. During crunch times, tensions there tended to run rather high.

On this particular Friday afternoon, the software engineering team was recovering from having pulled an all-nighter to complete a program update for an existing client. Most had left the office around 3:00 to catch up on about 24 hours of lost sleep. As a result, none of the eight of their group came to the meeting. This was unfortunate because our boss, who was also our director of sales, had an important announcement to make: he had just signed a deal with a major multinational corporation that would bring our company a million dollars over the next four years.

Our boss was quite upset about the absence of the software team. He thought their failure to attend the meeting was disrespectful to the rest of us, and he expressed his dismay in no uncertain terms.

"I am furious about this," he said. "Absolutely furious."

The room fell silent. We all stared at our shoes, unwilling to say anything for fear of making him even madder.

It seemed wrong to me, though, that our boss should be upset. I had been with the software engineering team until about 8:00 the previous evening. I knew how hard they were working. Disrespect for the rest of us was the last thing on their minds; they simply wanted to provide our client with the best service possible.

On the other hand, I had doubts about speaking up. I certainly didn't want to get my boss any angrier than he already was. And besides, perhaps he had a point; after all, *we* were all working hard, too, and *we* all made the meeting.

What helped me figure out the right thing to do was to think about what it meant to be a virtuous employee. I believed that the primary qualities I ought to embody were creativity, courage, and good judgment. These were in support of my core values: learning, teamwork, truth, and knowledge. A creative, courageous, and per-spicacious employee would, I believed, answer all seven of the moral spectrum questions in the same way: I would stand up for what I believed best facilitated our organization's excellence—even at the risk of alienating my boss.

So I spoke up. I told him that I thought he had no right to be furious at the software team, and that it was unfair to us to express his anger in this way; if he had a complaint about the software team's behavior, he ought to tell them, not us.

Initially, my boss was quite upset, but as it turned out, his ire was based in large part on being uninformed about the facts of the situation. He was extremely uncomfortable being so "out of the loop" on the software team's activities. Once he understood why they hadn't attended the meeting, though, he was somewhat mol-lified. He still didn't like the idea of their unilateral decision not to attend, but at least he saw their rationale. As he calmed down and the meeting progressed, he apologized for getting so worked up and thanked me for confronting him about his anger. He even held me up to the group as an example of how we ought to relate honestly to one another.

So in this case, things worked out. The right thing to do matched with the self-interested thing to do. Granted, I had to take some extra heat; but that heat was consistent with my values and the virtues by which those values were best expressed.

Of course, there's no guarantee that things will always have such a happy ending. However, the alternative—denying my principles to avoid conflict with my organizational superior—was no alternative at all. It was better to gamble on a possible positive outcome than accept the status quo—even if that status quo was safe and secure.

Loyalty Issues: What's Mine Is Mine, What's Yours Is Mine, Too

A third area of ethical risk that often emerges for businesspeople has to do with issues of loyalty, noncompetition, and technology transfer, especially where proprietary information is involved. And as more employees feel a greater sense of loyalty to their skills and education than to their companies, this will only increase. For example, software engineers who hone their programming abilities working for company X may have no qualms about moving to company Y—or starting their own company Z—where they make major contributions to their new organization's success by using information their old company directly or indirectly paid for. These technical experts probably have no intention to cheat their former employer—indeed, no sense that they are taking unfair advantage—but clearly, company X has a right to be concerned. So what is acceptable behavior, both on their parts and on their organization's? Should companies be permitted to constrain an individual's intellectual capital in some way? Should individuals require themselves to "forget" what they know in the interest of fair play?

Consider the case of my friend Tyler, a hotshot programmer in the multimedia gaming industry. Though just barely 30, Tyler had already worked for half a dozen companies in a handful of different new technologies. His career had mirrored the increasing sophistication of the gaming platforms on which he worked. With every new hardware development, from 8-bit to 32-bit to 64-bit machines, Tyler found for himself a new, more challenging, and more technically complex job. Each time, he brought his vast experience to bear on the problems facing this latest and greatest state-of-the-art technology. Of course, he always signed noncompete agreements with his employers, but it was his belief that they hardly applied. After all, every new job represented a new delivery platform. It wasn't as if the latest technology was really competing with the earlier one. Rather, it was an emerging market being developed. And besides, as far as his work was concerned, there was virtually no overlap. For each new system, new code had to be written. He couldn't just "cut and paste" what he had done previously, so while the applicable *experience* may have been gained while he was employed by someone else, the *results* of that experience—the actual lines of software code—weren't applicable at all. Whatever he created for his new employer was, in fact, new.

Until now. Now, for the first time in his career, Tyler was faced with a real question of intellectual property rights. And he didn't quite know what to do.

The problem was that Tyler's work in the last few years had shifted from developing software titles—the computer games and simulations themselves—to creating software tools—the applications that software developers working on titles used to build them. He had an opportunity now, having been approached by an industry headhunter, to move to a new company that intended to focus solely on the creation of such tools. They wouldn't compete directly with the gaming companies; rather, they would supply them with resources for creating their products more efficiently.

It sounded like a great job to Tyler; the company was a well-funded start-up with very cool offices that were half an hour closer to his home than his current workplace. The only wrinkle had to do with how much of his current experience as a tool developer the new company seemed to be counting on. When he talked with the senior developer on the phone—the guy who would be his boss—it sounded as if he was going to be expected to pretty much re-create what he had made for his current company. "Everyone knows that the tools you guys use are some of the best," he said. "If we have essentially the same thing in our hip pocket from the get-go, we'll be way ahead of the game."

Tyler felt a certain loyalty to his current company, but the new venture was attractive, too. What should he do?

Asking the seven moral prism questions helped, but he remained somewhat confounded. Egoism and existentialism told him unequivocally to go for it. Virtue ethics—considering that the most virtuous person Tyler could think of was a software engineer who had recently jumped ship to form his own competing start-up company—also suggested that he take the new job. The utilitarian, communitarian, and deontological moral prisms led him, for reasons of overall happiness, community standards, and duty to say no. And the ethic of caring prism left him torn: if he considered the relationship with his current company, he ought not leave; if he thought about the new one, it seemed he should.

What ultimately enabled him to decide what he ought to do was to think about the alignment of his values and virtues.

In his work, Tyler's primary values were technology, change, and excitement. The virtues he regularly tried to embody to support those values were creativity and determination. But it seemed as if his new company were emphasizing the virtues of speed and competitiveness instead. While these were virtues that Tyler admired, they weren't those he held in highest esteem. So, in the end, he decided to stay with his current company. The deciding factor was that their virtue—*how* they worked toward their goals—better aligned with Tyler's values—*what* those goals, in essence, were.

Here then, we have another example of how examining the alignment between values and virtues provides one more way of discovering the right thing to do. In particular, this case shows us how a tension between the two reveals to us that what we're doing isn't right. The claim isn't that such a disconnect *alone* settles the issue, but that taken in consideration with what our moral prisms tell us, the misalignment can give us a clearer sense of what actions we ought to avoid. In the end, it's all about expanding our moral palette, and this is one more way to do it—a way that may be especially useful for businesspeople who regularly find themselves having to deal with conflicting viewpoints.

But then, will this be sufficient for settling any and all ethical questions that arise on the job? Of course not. Contemporary business is far too complex and ever-changing for a purely formulaic approach to dealing with such issues. However, having a repertoire of principles at one's disposal is likely to lead to more sophisticated solutions that satisfy a more diverse constituency of customers, co-workers, and colleagues.

The principle we've explored here—that alignment between virtues and values helps point out to us what we ought to do—enriches our moral palette. And the richer our moral palette, the richer the results we can achieve.

Enough Is Enough: The Virtue of Temperance

Bertrand Russell said, "It is preoccupation with possession, more than anything else, that prevents men from living freely and nobly." In many ways, this is true. Our desires for the newest and brightest technologies, for more and better toys, keep us trapped in an endless cycle of acquisition and occupation. We're working overtime to pay off the bills for the mountains of stuff we already have. But because our lives feel so empty—since all we're doing is working—we try to fill that emptiness with possessions, and the cycle starts all over again.

For businesspeople, the situation is rife with irony. We are making things we want other people to want and the more they want them, the better we do. Naturally, we'd like our customers to crave what *we* make, but, at a certain level, we'd like to be free from those cravings ourselves. We don't want to be so programmed; we'd like to be able to rise above the persuasions of others. Ironically, most of us do our jobs too well. And as a consequence, we find ourselves besotted with desire, driven in our actions not by an interest in *doing* the right thing, but by an interest in *acquiring* the right thing.

The problem is that our appetites are out of control. We're too hungry for the next thing, and even when we get it, we're still not satisfied. One way of thinking about this is that we've lost touch with a virtue that the ancient Greeks knew all about, a state of character Plato calls *sophrosune*. Literally meaning something like "sound-minded," *sophrosune* is usually translated as "temperance," but it's more than that. It's the virtue associated with our appetites, the virtue that is exhibited by having the right desires for the right things at the right times.

People who are temperate are not ascetics. They have a healthy appetite for food, drink, sex, and other sensual pleasures. What's special about them, though, is that they want only the appropriate amount. They don't crave more than they need. And they don't have to *control* their appetites—they simply don't have a hunger for excess. In fact, if someone does have to rein in his desires, that is, if he wants more but forces himself not to indulge, then he doesn't really have the temperate virtue.

Most of us can probably go a long way in our development of *sophrosune*. We have much to learn about training our desires so we don't really want what we really don't want. Of course, it's not easy, especially since all around us are messages telling us we ought to want more—more power, more speed, more money, more bonus miles, more *more*. Advertisers, media, and the Joneses next door constantly prod our every desire, blurring the line between our needs and our wants. It becomes hard to tell where our desires end and where the desires other people desire us to desire begin. Developing an appetite for the right amount of power, speed, money, bonus miles, or whatever is especially difficult, since our internal standard for that amount is constantly being messed with. As soon as we think we're satisfied, the next version of the next big thing comes along and suddenly, we're supposed to be starving again—even though we've barely touched what we have. It makes one wonder whether there are any limits, whether developing *sophrosune* is even possible at all.

Another great Greek philosopher, Zorba, tells of one way to go about it. The hero of the Nikos Kazantzakis novel named after him,

Zorba explains to his "boss" how he cured himself of his appetite for cherries.

> "When I have a longing for something myself," he said, "do you know what I do? I cram myself chockful of it, and so I get rid of it and don't think about it any longer. Or, if I do, it makes me retch. Once when I was a kid—this'll show you—I was mad on cherries. I had no money, so I couldn't buy many at a time, and when I'd eaten all I could buy I still wanted more. Day and night I thought of nothing but cherries. I foamed at the mouth; it was torture. But one day I got mad, or ashamed, I don't know which. Anyway, I just felt cherries were doing what they liked with me and it was ludicrous. So what did I do? I got up one night, searched my father's pockets and found a silver *mejidie* and pinched it. I was up early the next morning, went to a market gardener and bought a basket o' cherries. I settle down in a ditch and begin eating . I stuffed and stuffed till I was all swollen out. My stomach began to ache and I was sick. Yes, boss, I was thoroughly sick, and from that day to this I've never wanted a cherry. I couldn't bear the sight of them. I could say to any cherry: I don't need you any more."[7]

Now, of course, not all our appetites lend themselves to Zorba's strategy. If it's money we're hungry for, we can't just run out to the store and purchase three packs of twenties. We obviously can't satisfy our desire by indulging in the object of desire. But perhaps we can achieve some satisfaction by indulging in the desire itself. Perhaps if we let ourselves be consumed by the desire it will eventually run its course. There's no guarantee this will happen, but it's not unheard of. No doubt we've all had the experience of wanting something with all our might but then one day waking up and finding that it no longer compels us. For some time a couple of years ago, I just *had* to have a new laptop. Every day I pored over Internet sites, looking at my options. I'd fantasize about all the new

---

[7]Katzanzakis, Nikos, *Zorba the Greek* (New York: Simon & Schuster, 1953), p. 195.

features I'd get and how people on airplanes would envy my way snazzy productivity tool.

But after weeks of indulging in my desire to get one, the desire just sort of burned itself out. Although I still wouldn't have minded a new model, I no longer ached for one. My desire for a better laptop hadn't been fulfilled, but the desire itself had abated. So it seems to me that sometimes it is possible to satisfy our desires for something not through the object of the desire but through the desire itself. And if this is the case, then our ability to achieve the virtue of *sophrosune* is never quite out of our reach.

And if this is the case, we can turn our attention away from business and to an area of our lives in which it is often even more difficult to determine the right thing to do: personal relationships.

Chapter Four

Right in Love

Doing Right by Friends, Family Members, and Loved Ones

Positive Negative Space

Our moral legacy will be distinguished primarily by the manner in which we have treated others. Most of our moral obligations— some would say *all*—are obligations to other people. Doing the right thing, therefore, is going to be mainly a matter of doing right by those we come in contact with on a regular basis: our friends, family members, loved ones, and colleagues.

But what makes it difficult to consistently treat others as we ought to treat them is that, often, our interests conflict. We want one thing, they want something else; or we both want the same thing at the same time and there's not enough to go around. Balancing these conflicting interests and coming up with mutually satisfying solutions requires a creative sensitivity that's hard to achieve. Lots of times, we get so wrapped up in our own needs and desires that we're unable to appreciate different perspectives—perspectives that may enable us to do a better job of fulfilling our interpersonal obligations.

All of us know what it feels like to be treated right by someone else. And, unfortunately, we all know what it feels like to be done wrong, too. But at least this means that we all have the necessary experience to distinguish between the two. The challenge, of course, is to determine what choices will ensure that the people we interact with will have the former, not the latter experience. Our moral legacy, after all, is in their hands. Its shape will ultimately be defined by their reactions to our treatment of them.

The great Russian author and playwright, Anton Chekhov, is said to have defined his characters by the manner in which others related to them. Any person on stage—or in life—was seen as the sum total of the responses his or her behavior evoked. Actors performing Chekhov would be urged to refrain from *presenting* their characters; rather, they would be encouraged to let the character *emerge* from the other characters' reactions. Our moral legacy is like that, too. We might think of it as being formed by the negative space around it, as opposed to the positive space it takes up. Think of the last puzzle piece in a puzzle. We know exactly what it looks like before we ever put it in place. Conceptualizing it is not very difficult; finding it, however, often is.

Finding the behaviors that will make our moral legacy fit into life's overall puzzle can be similarly challenging. That challenge is met, though, by determining the right thing to do in our day-to-day interactions with our fellow human beings. And that means being a good partner, colleague, parent, child, and—as many of us learn rather late in the game—a good friend.

With Friends Like This, Who Needs Friends?

I'm six years old, and Duncan Wilcox says he will be my best friend if I stick my finger in a garter snake's mouth. It seems a very small price to pay. I idolize Duncan. He is worldly (a second-grader!), strong (can pick me up and helicopter me around), and wise (knows all the best places to find crayfish in our local stream). I would do anything to make him like me: crawl through broken glass, take a bullet in the belly, climb into scary Mr. Miercord's yard to retrieve a lost ball. So, when we catch the snake and Duncan issues the dare, I don't hesitate.

Duncan holds the reptile's mouth open and I slide my index finger inside. The startled snake clamps down hard. I scream and dance around, waving my hand wildly, cracking the snake like a whip in an hysterical attempt to get it to let go. Finally, Duncan gets his hand on its tail. He pulls, the snake comes free, and I run home crying.

My mom calls the pediatrician, Dr. Michaels, to ask him if we need to come to the emergency room. "David put his finger in a garter snake's mouth," she explains. "Do you think we should worry about it?"

"His finger? No," replies Dr. Michaels calmly. "But his head—there we have a concern. What's going on in there that he should be so foolish?"

What Dr. Michaels can't see is how perfectly reasonable my decision to feed the snake my digit really is. Most of us are willing to bear much more than a nip on the finger by a non-poisonous reptile to earn the love and respect of those we love and respect. If Duncan keeps his promise to be my best friend, the pain and fear I am feeling will be well worth it.

Unfortunately, Duncan doesn't hold up his end of the bargain. That's why, a couple weeks later, when he says he'll be my best friend if I jump into the giant mud bog created by the installation of new sewer lines in our neighborhood, I literally leap at that chance, too. My feet sink in to over the tops of my cowboy boots. In order to free me, my Dad has to come pull me out with a rope tied under my armpits. The cowboy boots are lost forever and are probably still out there, stopping up drains in the suburbs of Pittsburgh to this day.

Once again, no one understands why I did it. "Why in heaven's name did you do such a silly thing, you silly child?" asks my mom as she scrubs mudballs from my ears and nostrils.

I try to explain that Duncan will be my best friend, but I can't make her see.

"That's ridiculous," she says. "A best friend would never ask you to do such things. A best friend is someone who cares about you as much as he cares about himself. And since I don't see Duncan jumping into the mud or putting his finger into the snake's mouth, I can't possibly see that he qualifies."

She is right, of course. Duncan will never be my best friend, in spite of my continuing attempts to win his favor. In subsequent months, I drink a shot glass full of Tabasco sauce, ride my wagon no-hands down the steepest hill in the neighborhood, and smack a hornet's nest with a broomstick, but to no avail—other than rivers of tears on my part.

And as a matter of fact, as long as Duncan continued to issue these tests for his friendship, my dreams of being his best buddy were doomed to failure. Mom had hit the proverbial nail on the head: Duncan wasn't acting like a friend at all; he wasn't treating me the right way for a friend to treat a friend.

Ironically, I had a best friend all this time and didn't even realize it. My next door neighbor, Timmy Short, who was a few months younger than me, was the antithesis of Duncan. Never once did he put conditions upon our friendship. Never once did he require me to demonstrate my worthiness by risking life and limb. Never once was I expected to be his source of amusement, where that amusement was not very amusing to me.

Instead, Timmy was genuinely interested in my well-being. He cared about me—for my sake, not his—and demonstrated his concern openly.

Six-year-olds are generally not known for their selflessness; Timmy, however, was entirely willing to consider my needs on a par with his own.

One time I was sick—nothing life threatening, just the sort of low-grade fever and general malaise that settles upon children.

Mostly it manifested itself in a heightened sense of neediness. I clung to my mother's waist and whimpered a lot, making more than my usual number of requests to be held and fed.

Timmy came by, and since I wasn't contagious, was allowed to stay. I clung on him and whimpered a lot, but he didn't seem to mind. We played doctor and patient, which was more like master and servant. Basically, I lay on my bed and asked him to fetch me things. He did so tirelessly and without complaining. When it came time for him to go home for lunch, I cried. He called up his mom and asked to stay the rest of the afternoon. We had so much fun playing that I completely forgot I was sick.

Now, who wouldn't say that Timmy was a better friend than Duncan? Who wouldn't agree that the kind of things he did were the right things for a real friend to do? Who wouldn't prefer to have a friend like Timmy than one like Duncan?

And if the answers to these questions are so obvious, isn't it equally obvious that there are better and worse ways for friends to treat each other? So by clarifying what these are, it seems to me that we can develop principles that apply to all our personal relationships: friends, lovers, family members, even casual acquaintances and perfect strangers.

Not that this is anything new; Aristotle trod this same road some 2500 years ago; we can retrace his steps a bit to get a better sense of where we've come from and where we're going.

The Virtue of Friendship

According to Aristotle, there are three kinds of friendship, corresponding to the three kinds of reasons we have for finding things lovable. Friendship, like our love for things, is based on one of three factors: utility, pleasure, or the good.

Friendships based on utility depend on both parties getting something from each other. We all have friends like these; there's nothing wrong with it as long as both parties are aware of what's going on. My friendship with my barber is kind of like this. When we're together, we each get something out of it. He fills me in on the latest neighborhood gossip; I provide him with an attentive and responsive audience. I get a good haircut; he gets a satisfied paying customer. In the broadest sense, he's useful to me and I am to him, too. Our friendship is founded on mutual benefit, and we're both aware of that. Were we not getting something we need from each other out of the relationship, it wouldn't continue.

And it's not just customer/client relationships that represent this type of friendship. Some of my friendships with colleagues are utility-based. We use each other to bounce ideas around. Our affection for each other—which is quite real—is nonetheless based on the benefit we receive. We're not so much concerned about what the other party gets out of the friendship; rather, we're in it for our own sake. Again, this isn't to suggest that we're not actually friends. We are. It's just that the reason we're friends is self-interested. But since everyone is aware of this, it's not a problem.

The second kind of friendship Aristotle identifies is one based on pleasure. Again, this should be quite familiar to us. Who doesn't have at least one friend whom we see only at parties or special events and whom we like because he or she makes us laugh? My friend Andrew is this kind of friend. I've never been to his house. I'm not even sure what he does for a living. But everytime we run into each other, we have a great time. He totally cracks me up and I do the same for him. At a party, we stand near the punchbowl, toasting one another and trading stories. I always have a blast in his company, but it doesn't go any further than that. Both of us are interested only in the pleasure we derive from the relationship. It's not as if we don't care about each other, it's just that our affection is based on the pleasant feelings we get when we're together. I'm glad, in the end, that Andrew has a good time when he's with me, but that's secondary to *my* having a good time. If he stopped enjoying my company, I could still be friends with him. If I stopped enjoying his, I wouldn't hang out with him anymore.

The third type of friendship—and, for Aristotle, the highest type—is where both friends wish well for each other for each other's own sake. These are friendships based on the good, where that good is what's good for the friend. Loving another is the essence of this experience, rather than being loved. Such friendships are rare but they are the most permanent, transcending distance, time, and circumstance. Most of us can count ourselves fortunate to have one or two such friends in our lives. If we're lucky, our spouse or life partner is this kind of friend. Traditional wisdom says that men have fewer of this type of friend than women do, and given that many men find it difficult to put the interests of others before their own, this may be true.

In any case, men and women alike don't easily make this kind of friend. For some of us, such friendships are forged only rather early in life; by the time we have families and responsibilities, there's no time for building and sustaining this rarest and most valuable kind of friendship. And this is a great shame, because all of us hunger for friends of this type. Aristotle reminds us that friendships based on the good are a necessary component of an authentically happy life.

He also reminds us why it's so difficult to develop this highest form of friendship. Because such relationships are based on an authentic concern for the other person's well-being, only good people can experience them. Bad people do not delight in each other unless some advantage comes of the relationship. Only good people, who for Aristotle will be people whose character is virtuous, can derive pleasure from another person's good.

It makes sense then, that in the interest of such good, meaningful, and life-sustaining relationships, we explore a little more carefully what it means to be a good person and, especially, a good friend. What, in other words, is the right thing to do in our relationships with others? What makes a right act toward someone else right? And how do we tell?

Learning the Hard Way, or
Do As I Say, Not As I Do

Suppose you've turned your house upside-down looking for your car keys, but still haven't found them. At this point, the best strategy may to be begin looking in places you're sure they're not. You probably won't find them there, but at least you'll narrow down possibilities and begin to sketch the outline of where they have to be. The same principle is applied to the discovery of good relationships in the example that follows.

It's the end-of-the-year party in Mrs. Hyman's seventh-grade homeroom. We've all brought goodies from home. Cookies and cake, brownies, and fudge bars have been spread out over the big worktables on which students usually do art projects. Mrs. Hyman has supplied a huge bowl of bright red cherry Kool-Aid™ to wash it all down.

The party is winding up. And "wound up" is also the right way to describe all of us: a classroom of 12- and 13-year-olds sugar-rushing to the max on the trays of sweets we've just consumed.

The girls are clustered on one side of the room giggling and whispering. The boys, including me, are slouched together on the other side, smirking and scoffing. None of us has the foggiest idea of what the girls could be talking about, but we don't let on. The pudgy Max Monrovic floats his conjecture.

"Alexandra Scoulas loves you, Shapiro. Look at how she covers her mouth when she looks at you. I read in this book called *Body Language* that that's a sure sign."

"You're full of it. It's you she loves." I poke Max in his ample stomach. "She told me her favorite food is Butterball turkey."

"If you're talking to her about favorite foods, that proves you love her!" exclaims Charles Titterington, punching me on the shoulder for emphasis.

I spin around and clench my fists like a tough guy. "Do not! I hate girls. And Alexandra Scoulas most of all!"

A sly smile creases Charles' face. "Oh yeah? Prove it."

I don't feel a pressing need to respond until Max chimes in. "Yeah, prove it, Scoulas-lover."

"Okay, then I will." I huddle us closer together. "Here's the plan. I go over there holding a full glass of punch. You guys come by and jostle me and I'll spill it all over her."

Charles guffaws. "No way. You're chicken."

"Of what?" I ask, stealing a glance at the girls. "You think Scoulas can take me?"

"Of Hyman," says Max. "She busts you, you're suspended from school."

"How's she gonna bust me? It's gonna totally be an accident. I'll bet if I grab some paper towels and start cleaning the floor, she thanks me and says how helpful I am."

Apparently, I convince them because a couple of moments later, we're all standing near Alexandra Scoulas, ostensibly scouting around for any remaining goodies. I sidle up to her, holding my juice cup near my chest. Charles and Max pretend to fight over the last fudge bar. Charles grabs it away, Max lunges, brushing my arm. "Hey!" I exclaim, and in slow-motion, the cup flies out of my hand. It lands squarely on Alexandra Scoulas' chest, emptying its crimson contents all down the front of her white shirt.

She bursts into tears. I complain that I was bumped. It was an accident, I announce loudly to anyone within earshot.

Mrs. Hyman comes over, armed for bear. "What's going on here?" she demands to know.

I quickly explain how the accident occurred. I ask for some paper towels to start cleaning up the mess.

It all unfolds just as I predicted. Mrs. Hyman commends me for being so helpful. She takes Alexandra out of the room to comfort her and clean off her shirt. None of them—not even Alexandra herself—ever suspects me of having planned what happened.

After school, Charles and Max congratulate me in the playground.

"I can't believe you pulled it off," says Charles, slapping me a high-five. "When I saw that juice flying, I thought you were busted for sure."

"Yeah, I was all ready for Hyman to take you down to the principal," adds Max. "Especially when Scoulas started crying."

I look at both of them like they're speaking a foreign language. "What are you guys talking about? Why should I have gotten taken down to the principal? It was an accident. You guys bumped me, I spilled the cup. Not my fault."

"But you planned the whole thing," says Max.

"So? I plan lots of things. Am I supposed to get busted for that?"

Charles squints at me, as if he's seeing a whole new—and infinitely more cool—person in front of him. I kind of like the feeling. "But you did her wrong," he says, drawing out the word "wrong" like a Delta blues singer.

"That's where you're wrong, Charles," I say, tapping him on the chest. "I didn't do anything wrong at all. Nothing at all. It wasn't my fault."

But of course it was my fault. I *did* do something wrong. Something mean. So mean that when I think about it now, I literally cringe. I treated Alexandra awfully. I destroyed her blouse, but far worse than that, I used her as a way to prop up my reputation with Charles and Max. I treated her as if she were a lifeless thing rather than a human being with authentic thoughts and feelings. For all I cared, she could have been a mannequin that I spilled juice on to show my buddies how cool I was.

Kant would give a rather straightforward explanation for why my behavior toward Alexandra was wrong. He would say that I was treating her only as a means to an end rather than an end in herself. Kant says we have a duty to respect the dignity of rational beings—humans—and that failure to respect this dignity ultimately represents a failure to respect one's own dignity. It is morally wrong to treat people only as a means to the satisfaction of our own desires because doing so denies not only their humanity, but our own, as well.

Remember that in the first formulation of his famous "categorical imperative," Kant admonishes us to act only in ways whereby we can at the same time will that the maxim of our action be universal law. Once again, he's saying that we need to examine our motives and see whether in a world where everyone acted on such motives, they would be self-defeating. But this sounds like a pretty complicated bit of mental gymnastics. Suppose I try to imagine everyone on earth saying to themselves something like, "Whenever I want to impress my friends, I will spill cherry soda on someone." Presumably, Kant would say that this motive is self-defeating because, in such a world, there would be no such thing as friends. How could there be when anyone is apt to spill cherry soda on you at any moment?

It's much easier, therefore, to apply Kant's second version of the categorical imperative. Here he says that we must act so as to treat humanity, whether in our own person or in that of any other, in every case as an end, and never as a means only. It's pretty plain to see that I didn't treat Alexandra as an end; I *used* her entirely as a means to achieve something I wanted for myself. I didn't care what her needs and desires were; I acted as if she had none. By extension, therefore, I acted as if I had none either. Clearly, by Kant's lights then, what I did was wrong.

But is Kant right in assuming that treating someone else as a means is tantamount to treating oneself as a means, too? I think he is, and the reason is to be found in a principle that's much simpler and more familiar than any Kant himself proposed: the Golden Rule.

The Golden Rule says that we should treat others as we would have them treat us. It follows naturally, then, that if we say it's okay to treat others as a means, then it's okay for them to treat us as a means, too. Implicit in my willingness to disrespect Alexandra's humanity was a willingness to have her disrespect mine, too.

Certainly, though, one could ask why this is wrong. If, after all, I'm okay with being treated as a means, why should it be wrong for me to treat others in that way, too? This is a famous objection to the Golden Rule. Masochists, for instance, might want to be treated awfully by others. Wouldn't it be okay for them to treat others awfully, too?

What this objection misses, however, is the sense of what it means to be treated as one would have others treat you. Granted, masochists might want to be treated poorly, but they still want to be treated as *they* want. They want their ends to be respected. This means they aren't privileged to treat others as masochists want to be treated; they must treat others as *those people* themselves want to be treated. Now, if they happen to be masochists, too, then presumably it's okay to make them suffer. But since most people aren't interested in experiencing pain, masochists aren't permitted to inflict it on others—even though they wouldn't mind having pain inflicted on them.

What emerges from this is a renewed appreciation for the Golden Rule as a way to help us determine the right thing to do. Consider it a further expansion of our moral palette, another moral prism through which to examine the world. It can, perhaps, be a tiebreaker in cases where no clear answer is found among the utilitarian, deontological, communitarian, and virtue ethics perspectives. Moreover, when it comes to interpersonal relationships, it may well be the most appropriate perspective to take, independent of other considerations.

At least it was for me, one time some years ago when I was trying to figure out the right thing to do to end a romantic relationship.

[*FADE IN:* HOLLYWOOD, EARLY 1980'S. INTERIOR—MY APARTMENT.]

Your typical first apartment: a futon couch, cinder-block bookshelves, an impressive stereo dominating the living room. I share this place with my girlfriend of about three years, Rita. Or, to be more precise, I have *been sharing* it with her; as soon as I can, I'm moving out. I've come to this decision over the course of the last week. Rita's been away visiting friends in San Francisco. I've been in Hollywood, enjoying the single life. Not that this has entailed anything particularly wild or woolly; the enjoyment has stemmed primarily from not having to keep trying to breathe life into a dying relationship.

Rita and I have drifted apart in our years together; she is deeply into her life as production manager for a motion picture sound studio; I am busy trying to make a living writing jokes for stand-up comedians. We hardly ever see each other, and when we do, it's fairly tense. Last month, in a fit of pique, she threw a bowl of cooked noodles at me. It missed, but since neither of us were willing to break down and clean up the mess, the noodles stayed stuck on the wall for weeks, hardening to a lacquered sheen.

[*DISSOLVE TO:* INTERIOR—MY CAR.]

I'm on my way to pick Rita up at the Burbank airport. I've resolved to tell her of my decision to move out as soon as I see her. I believe this is the right thing to do because this is what I would want if I were in her shoes. No sense in pretending our affair is fine. We both know our lives can't go on as they've been. It's time to make a clean breast of things; anyway, we'll always be friends.

[*DISSOLVE TO:* INTERIOR—THE AIRPORT.]

Rita is heading down the jetway to greet me. She is all smiles. The past week has had an entirely opposite effect on her view of our relationship. She has missed me and wants to reconcile. In her mind's eye, this evening is going to be an opportunity to reconnect and make plans for our future together. She has even brought a special peace offering: two cartons of my favorite food, hot and sour vegetables from the place the New Yorker magazine calls the "best Chinese restaurant in the world," Hunan Restaurant in San Francisco.

As she enters the terminal, she holds the two containers of Chinese food before her. "Look what I brought you!" she exclaims. "Straight from Hunan. Still hot."

The heady fragrance of the stir-fried vegetables and chile peppers snakes into my nostrils. I very nearly swoon with pleasure.

Rita takes my reaction to be directed at her. She leans in for a hug. "I'm so glad to see you, sweetheart. Did you miss me?"

Suddenly, I'm faced with a quandary. If I tell her the truth, she's going to be furious. My two cartons of hot and sour vegetables will likely suffer the same fate as last month's noodles. Am I willing to make nice for at least long enough to enjoy my dinner? Or should I go through with my original resolve to tell Rita the truth right away? As is usually my strategy in such cases, I waffle, postponing a choice. "Here, let me take your bag," I answer, reaching for the daypack Rita has slung around her shoulders. "I'm parked illegally. We need to hurry."

[*DISSOLVE TO:* INTERIOR—MY CAR.]

On the way back to Hollywood, Rita chats cheerfully about her week in San Francisco. She says she had a good time visiting friends, but that the whole time she was there, she kept thinking of me. She was surprised how much she missed me and really wants to get to know me all over again. As she talks, the scent of hot and sour vegetables fills the car. I can practically taste the pungent flavor of those crisp cabbage leaves and carrot slices. It takes all my willpower to keep from pulling over and digging into the cartons right away. I try to concentrate on navigating the freeway traffic, using that as an excuse to appear distracted when Rita asks me questions.

[*DISSOLVE TO:* INTERIOR—MY APARTMENT.]

I follow Rita into the kitchen, setting her bag down by the door. She puts the two cartons of Chinese food on the kitchen table, and turns, opening her arms wide to me. "Come give me a hug. Then let's have some dinner."

I look at Rita's open arms, and then at the closed containers of food. I almost take a step toward her, but then I stop. I think about this.

I think about it in utilitarian terms. As far as maximization of total happiness goes, I ought to go ahead and hug her, refrain from telling her of my decision, and enjoy the dinner. Short-term, at least, we'll both be much happier.

I gaze through the communitarian moral prism. Even if everyone I know knew what I was doing, I'd be perfectly comfortable postponing the breakup until after we eat.

Same goes for the virtue ethics perspective: The most virtuous person I know of at the time—my punk-rock impresario friend, Larry Livermore—would definitely have gone for the Chinese food. He was the one who turned me on to Hunan in the first place and considered it almost a spiritual sacrament. For that matter, Aristotle himself would hardly have objected. The Greeks, after all, recognized the healthy enjoyment of food and drink as a sign of virtuous character. So as long as I don't go overboard and eat both cartons in a single sitting, it would seem that choosing dinner is the right thing to do.

The existentialist prism tells me to maximize our freedom. Being free to enjoy dinner seems to fall naturally under that admonition, so I ought to keep quiet about my intentions until after we eat. Egoism urges me to enjoy the food because that's what I want. The ethic of caring prism suggests I ought to sustain the caring relationship between Rita and me as long as possible; certainly I ought to do so until we've cleared our plates.

Not even the Kantian prism presents any obvious challenge to putting off telling Rita how I feel. Imagine a world in which everyone did so. It's not as if there's anything manifestly contradictory about deciding to eat first in that world. Now, perhaps Kant would object on the grounds that I am using Rita as a means to an end, that is, the food. But since I'm not using her *solely* as an end—I am, after all, still interested in Rita's happiness and well-being—I believe I'm in the clear.

So, all things considered, it appears that I'm perfectly justified in keeping Rita in the dark so as to enjoy my meal.

I take another step toward Rita, but something stops me. In spite of the thought process I've just gone through, it still doesn't seem right to sweep the truth under the rug—or perhaps more appropriately, the tablecloth.

The reason comes to me when I consider things in light of the Golden Rule. Suppose I were in Rita's shoes. Would I want to sit down to a nice meal with someone who was hiding such vital information from me? The answer, in spite of my deep affection for hot and sour vegetables, would have to be "no." If I am to treat Rita as I would have her treat me, I have no choice but to disclose what I'm feeling, even if it means dinner will be ruined.

That's just what happens. As soon as I start to explain why I can't give her a hug, things go haywire. Soon, we're screaming at each other. The battle ends when Rita stomps open the garbage can and pours the two containers of Chinese food deep into its soggy interior. Well, not quite: it really ends when she storms from the room and slams herself shut in the bedroom, telling me to collect up my things and find someplace else to stay. She's keeping the apartment and I may as well get used to it.

I've prepared for this. I've got a cot set up in my office and can sleep there until I find a new apartment. I gather up my toothbrush, a couple changes of clothes, and my typewriter, and put them in my car. After a last tour of the apartment to make sure I'm not forgetting anything vital, I squat down by the kitchen garbage can. With the lid up, I can still smell the hot and sour vegetables, even though their fragrance is masked by the odor of rotting vegetables and stale coffee filters. Tentatively, I reach a hand inside, parting the garbage as delicately as I would open a rose petal. My fingers make contact with a stir-fried cabbage leaf. I withdraw it carefully and brush a few coffee grounds away. I put the cabbage in my mouth and just hold it there, letting the hot and sour sauce that clings to it seep around my tongue. I rise slowly and say good-bye to my home and farewell to the dinner that might have been. Only after I close the front door behind me do I begin chewing and swallow my meal.

So, did I do the right thing that night with Rita? Were I to answer based solely on consequences, as a utilitarian or, to a lesser degree, a virtue ethicist would, the answer would be a resounding "no." Not only did I lose out on dinner, I also hurt Rita's feelings, and got kicked out of my house. On balance, my decision to tell her the truth created a lot more pain than pleasure; consequentially, I ought not to have done it.

Nevertheless, it's clear to me that the choice I made was the right one. Anything else would have been deceptive. It would have been to use Rita as a meal ticket, to pretend I was willing to reconcile with her for the sole purpose of enjoying dinner.

This isn't to say that a bit of creative dissembling is *never* acceptable between partners. Sometimes a little white lie may be just the thing to save a person's feelings and grease the relationship's wheels. But in this case, my motivation was all wrong. It wasn't Rita's feelings I was concerned about, it was my appetite. If she hadn't shown up with the Hunan food, I never would have found myself in such a quandary. I would have told her how I felt right away—just as planned—and accepted the consequences. It wasn't until I had a vested interest in her satisfaction that my problem arose. And were I to put myself in her shoes, I would have to say that the only fair way to resolve that problem would be to put myself in her shoes. And since I'd feel awful being lied to for the price of dinner, then I ought not to do so to anyone else.

So here we can see how the Golden Rule, informed by our appreciation for a variety of moral perspectives, can point us in the right direction when it comes to relationships between partners. But what about between friends? Or family members? Or business associates?

Golden Friendships

There's something terribly ironic about the huge popularity of television programs like *Seinfield* and *Friends*. The shows feature stories about longtime friends whose lives are so deeply intertwined they spend nearly all their waking hours together. But, for the most part, they are watched by individuals sitting alone in their homes. Instead of having such complex and difficult relationships themselves, viewers participate in them vicariously. We watch people on

TV having the kind of friendships we wish we had. And what makes it even more ironic is that, to a great extent, the very reason we *don't* have such friendships is that we're camped out in front of the TV set. Rather than hanging with our real-life buddies, drinking coffee and hatching harebrained schemes, we're glued to the boob tube feeling bad that we don't have best pals like Kramer, George, and Elaine. And as a matter of fact, for many of us, Kramer, George, and Elaine are our best pals; after all, we spend a lot more time with them than we do with our living, breathing friends.

Oddly, I hardly know anyone who doesn't wish he or she had better friendships. It seems to be a symptom of what Dick Leider calls the "hurry sickness" of contemporary life. We're all rushing around, trying so hard to accomplish things, that we don't have time for friendships to grow. If we're lucky, we manage to keep in touch via e-mail or by leaving messages on each other's answering machines. Our friends become "virtual friends"; we carry on our relationships without ever seeing one another face-to-face. While this prevents us from feeling terribly isolated and alone, it's ultimately dissatisfying. We yearn for those long and lazy afternoons together listening to music, those late night conversations extending into dawn, those impromptu afternoon excursions to nowhere in particular. We yearn, in other words, for *real* friendships, neither vicarious nor virtual: the sort of friendships we had as kids or young adults, the sort of friendships that seem so difficult to forge later in life.

The students in Ms. Hutchings' sixth grade class at Whitman Middle School have these kinds of friends. They sit close together, four to a table, whispering, laughing, and passing notes while we do philosophy together.

I am here for two hours as I am every other week during the school year. During this time, we explore topics in ethics, epistemology, metaphysics, and logic by reading stories, doing exercises, and having freewheeling discussions that the students direct by asking questions and challenging nearly everything I say.

Today we are talking about friendship and how friends ought to treat each other. We have developed a number of hypothetical dilemmas to test our assumptions about what it means to be a friend.

"Suppose your friend asks you to cheat on a test," I ask. "What is the right thing to do?"

Chad, one of the brightest, most athletic, and popular kids in the class exclaims, "Let him cheat! It makes no difference to you, and, if he's your friend, you should help him."

Brenna, who initially was rather quiet and reserved but in recent weeks has emerged as one of the most articulate and persuasive talkers in class disagrees. "It's not helping him if you help him cheat, though. What if he has to take a test and you're not there? I mean, if you were him, wouldn't you rather know what you didn't know?"

"It depends on who the friend is," interjects Lea, a very funny girl whose perspective on things is usually as delightfully odd as her outfits. Today she is sporting a sort of retro-sixties ensemble, complete with dangly bracelets and hoop earrings. Her attitude is sort of retro-sixties in a counter-cultural way, too. "If it's a really good friend, then you should be willing to help him out no matter what. Tests don't really prove anything, anyway; it's not like you won't get a good job someday just because you don't know the capital of Nebraska; so why not help her?"

The conversation goes back and forth like this for a while, but in general students are sympathetic to letting their friend cheat. They tend to imagine themselves in the position of the cheater. "Think how you would feel if your friend cared more about some stupid test than about your friendship," says Amy, looking rather pointedly at her friends at their shared table. "I'm not sure I could still be friends with someone who was so petty."

From my perspective as a philosopher, I love the way the discussion is going. Students are making claims and offering arguments to support them. They're giving example and counterexamples and actually listening to what each other has to say.

From my perspective as a teacher, I'm appalled. None of the students seem particularly troubled at the prospect of cheating itself. Their concerns have only to do with the consequences of the act: what will happen to the friendship, whether the cheater will get caught, and so on.

I decide to shift gears and try a different dilemma. "Imagine that, for a joke, your best friend puts a whoopie cushion on the teacher's chair. Your teacher doesn't think it's very funny when she sits down and says that unless someone tells her who did it, the entire class will have to stay after school. Your friend is not going to admit it, and you're the only other person who knows. What is the right thing to do?"

A couple of students shoot their hands up immediately. One of them, Paul, who is probably the one most likely to do something like put a whoopie cushion on the teacher's chair, doesn't wait to be called on to speak. "You better not squeal! I would never squeal on my best friend; no best friend of mine would squeal on me."

Brenna agrees wholeheartedly. "The whole thing about being a best friend is that you do what each other wants. Maybe you'd try to talk your friend into admitting she did it, but if she didn't feel like telling, it would be totally wrong for you to do it for her. You have to think about what you would want her to do if you were in each other's place."

Since Brenna's eloquent answer pretty well sums up the way most of the students feel, I offer one more sample dilemma.

"Suppose you're spending the afternoon with a friend of yours who isn't very popular. You're out and about and run into a group of other friends—including your best friend—who are going to the movies. They have one extra free ticket and invite you to come along. Your unpopular friend, though, is not invited. What is the right thing to do?"

"What's the movie?" Paul wants to know.

The class boos. "What difference does that make?" shouts Amy.

"Just kidding," says Paul, somewhat contritely. "I'm not going to ditch my friend. Don't worry."

"You can see a movie anytime," explains Chad. "But you've made a promise to your friend to spend this time together and you only have this one chance to do so."

"Suppose it was a concert or something like that," suggests Lea, offering exactly the sort of philosophical challenge I was thinking of proposing, "something that only ran once."

"It still wouldn't be right to leave your friend." Steve, a quiet kid, who probably feels a certain affinity for the unpopular friend, adds his voice to the discussion. "Nobody deserves to be left behind just so you can go do something you'd rather do."

"Maybe you could talk to your friend and explain the situation," responds Chad. "Maybe you could arrange to do something later, after the concert, and then you could go."

"Sure you *could* do that," answers Brenna, unable or unwilling to hide the disdain in her voice. "But it would still be a completely sleazy thing to do. I mean how would you like it if your friend said to you 'I have something better to do right now than be your friend, so why don't you wait around until I'm done and then I'll let you hang with me some more'?"

"No friend of *mine* would say that to me," says Chad.

'That's just the point." Lea does a good job of summarizing the discussion. "No friend of *anyone's* would do that to them. Because if they did do that, they wouldn't be a friend."

As the students nod their heads in agreement, I am impressed with how clear a picture they have of the responsibilities and obligations that go along with friendship. At 11 and 12 years old, they have a better idea of what it means to be a true friend than many of us do at 41 or 52. Granted, their intense focus on the importance of loyalty has the potential to lead them somewhat astray—as in the cheating example—but this seems to be a function of a deeper appreciation for the very principle on which long-lasting friendships are founded. It's the principle we've been talking about: the Golden Rule.

Ms. Hutchings' students consistently address the question of how friends ought to treat each other by trying to put themselves in their friends' shoes. They wonder how they'd want to be treated themselves were the tables turned. Their test for what a friend should do is simple and elegant: treat your friends as you would have them treat you.

It's no wonder they have so much fun around their tables and hanging out after school with their friends. And it's no surprise that they don't spend their evenings watching *Seinfield* and *Friends*.

Golden Parents

What would it mean exactly to treat your kids as you would have them treat you? We obviously can't take this quite literally. In my case, this would imply that it would have been wrong for me to prevent my 1-year-old daughter from using the stove or walking across the street or from staying up past 10:00 at night. Since I would prefer that she didn't impose on me the sort of paternalistic restrictions I expect to be permitted to impose on her, it would seem, by the Golden Rule, that I ought not to do so. But this is ridiculous— as best attested to by the fact that, as teenagers, we often argued just this way when trying to negotiate a later curfew time from our parents or guardians.

Maybe the best we can do, therefore, is conceive of things in terms of mutual respect. What choices would do the best job of conveying a sense of shared respect between parents and children? How can I behave, I would ask, so that my daughter understands that my treatment of her is motivated entirely by an abiding respect for her as an individual? So that even when I do impose restrictions upon her that she finds overly constraining, she can see that the restrictions come out of a recognition that she has desires, goals, and needs that are unique from my own?

Were this a book exclusively on child-rearing, I might have more in-depth answers to these questions. And were I an expert on parent-child relationships instead of simply an enthusiastic student of them, I might be better able to provide a comprehensive program for ensuring mutual respect between parents and their kids.

As it is, the best I can do is offer an example of this kind of respect in action. As the child in this example, I must say I felt deeply respected by my parent's behavior. And, perhaps more to the point, I felt that I was being treated as my parent would have wanted to be treated were we in each others' shoes.

I'm 15 years old and, like all 15-year-olds, know everything about everything. What I care about, though, are just three things: my friends, my music collection, and my hair—especially my hair. As is the style of the day, I am growing it out. I want nothing more than to have a long "freak flag," to wave in the breeze as I "truck" around town. I want long locks to cover my face when I doze in class. Unfortunately, I attend a prep school with a dress code that limits the length of my tress. Students are prohibited from having hair that extends over the ears on the side or that goes beyond the base of the collar in back.

I know how to beat the system, though. My teachers and principal aren't as smart as I am; I can easily outwit them using my superior sophistication and cleverness. One Saturday, that sophistication and cleverness "enhanced" by a pipeful of marijuana, I devise a surefire plan to grow my hair down to my shoulders and have them be none the wiser.

I hop a bus downtown to "Walter's Wig World," advertised in the Yellow Pages as "Western Pennsylvania's largest purveyor of quality hairpieces for men and women." Walter, an elderly gentleman who pretty obviously sports one of his own wares, shows me around.

"So what are you looking for, exactly?" he inquires, sizing up my quite full head of hair.

I explain my plan to Walter. I need a short-hair wig to cover up my own lengthening locks. It has to be about the same color as my real hair and look entirely lifelike.

Walter is justifiably proud of the quality of his stock, but he is highly skeptical that my plan will work.

"With all that hair up under there," he says, pointing first to my head and then to the wig I've picked out, "there's no way the hairpiece is going to sit flush to your scalp. As fine a quality as this wig is, I don't think you're going to fool anyone that it's really your own hair."

As far as I'm concerned, old Walter doesn't know what he's talking about. Maybe I'm just stoned—I am—but the wig looks fine to me. Sure it rides a bit high, but no one at my school will notice. As clueless as my teachers are, they'll probably be asking me the name of my barber for a reference.

I pay forty bucks for the wig—all the money I have in the world. I ride the bus back home and stash my purchase in my sock drawer. A couple of times over the weekend, I get it out and try it on. Sunday evening, no longer under the influence of recreational stimulants, I'm less convinced it looks great. Still, my remarkably low estimation of my teachers' powers of discernment keeps me confident that they'll never notice.

Monday morning and with the help of about a dozen bobby pins and a couple of rubber bands, I get my hair tucked up underneath the wig. Needless to say, it's not very convincing. My hairstyle resembles a giant puff pastry of some sort—what the French call a brioche, maybe. It looks astonishingly similar to the "do" worn by the Big Boy hamburger chain mascot.

At breakfast, my dad takes one look at me and bursts out laughing. I glare at him. He just shakes his head and returns to his newspaper.

My mother examines me from her place by the stove. "You don't honestly think they're going to let you wear that wig in school, do you David?" she asks, pointing at its flaws with her spatula.

"What makes you think it's a wig?" I sneer.

My father fails to stifle a guffaw. My mother tries to answer me seriously. "Well, aside from it being at best the merest approximation of your actual hair color, the fact that it rides over your forehead like Dracula's outstretched cape tends to give it away a bit."

"You guys don't know anything," I assert. "I'll bet you five bucks that nobody says anything."

It's a good thing my parents don't take me up on my wager, otherwise, I'd be out five bucks. For no sooner do I walk into my school building than my English teacher, Mr. Trimble, grabs me by the shoulder. "Lose the wig, Shapiro."

"What wig?"

"All right, we're going to see Dr. Corrigan."

Trimble marches me into the headmaster's office. There things proceed rather quickly. Dr. Corrigan insists that I remove the wig. I feebly attempt another "what wig?" gambit. Trimble defuses that strategy by pulling the hairpiece off my head.

Dr. Corrigan calls my mom on the phone. He puts her on the speaker so I can hear—I assume he does this whenever he calls homes so students can know what big trouble they are in.

As soon as he identifies himself, my mom guesses the nature of Dr. Corrigan's call.

"It's about that silly wig, isn't it?" she asks.

Dr. Corrigan nods gravely. "Yes."

"Well, I told him it looked ridiculous," she says. "He wasn't going to fool anyone."

"You're aware that we have a policy about students' grooming," says Dr. Corrigan into the phone, giving me and my shaggy locks the once-over with his eyes.

"I am," says my mom. "Although I must admit I think it's rather petty in this day and age. Certainly there must be more important battles for educators to fight."

Dr. Corrigan isn't quite prepared for her editorial, so he pretends he hasn't heard. "You'll see to it, then, that David gets his hair cut?"

My mom refuses to be painted into a corner. "I will do my utmost to encourage him. He's a rather independent-minded child, in case you haven't noticed."

I think Dr. Corrigan is a little bit scared of my mom. He's so eager to get off the phone that he takes her somewhat measured response as a ringing endorsement of his request.

"You heard what she said," he says to me after he hangs up. "I expect to see you in full compliance with our dress code when you arrive here tomorrow."

I sigh the sort of world-weary sigh that is as ubiquitous among teenagers as pimples. "Sure." A pause, during which time it seems that Dr. Corrigan is waiting for me to express remorse or beg his forgiveness or something. I don't bite. "Can I go now?" I ask.

"Of course." Having won, Dr. Corrigan can afford to be gracious.

I stand and now I pause, waiting for him to make an offer. He doesn't bite either. "Can I have it?" I ask at length.

Dr. Corrigan apparently has no idea what I'm talking about.

"The wig," I say, pointing to the disheveled spider of hair on the edge of his desk.

"Take it," he says, gesturing expansively. "Just be sure you don't bring it back through the four walls of our academy."

I have no intention whatsoever of doing so. My only interest is in taking it back to "Walter's Wig World" and getting a refund. If I can't use the wig to overcome the primary source of my difficulties with school, at least I can use the money to buy something with which to help me alleviate the pain.

Unfortunately, this isn't an option. Walter himself gives me the bad news. "Sorry, kid. But we can't take back any hairpieces once they've left the store. State law. I'd love to help you, but my hands are tied."

Defeated again, I am positively fuming by the time I arrive home. I explode through the door and into the kitchen where my mother is eating toast and reading a detective novel. I throw the offending wig at her feet. "It's all your fault!" I cry. "If you didn't make me go to that stupid school, I never would have done it."

"Done what?" asks my mother.

"Bought that stupid wig!" I shout, giving the hairpiece a kick for emphasis. "Wasted all my money on it."

My mother rolls her eyes.

"You owe me!" I demand. "It's your fault I bought it. You owe me forty dollars!"

"Don't be silly." My mother returns to her novel.

"Yes you do. Forty dollars! Plus bus fare! You made me buy the wig and you should have to pay for it."

My mother puts down her book and faces me directly. "David," she says in a clear, cool voice, "no one made you buy that except yourself. You and your friends got stoned on marijuana and then you decided all by yourself to buy that wig. If you really think I am responsible for buying that wig, then that stuff you are smoking really has addled your brain."

For a moment, I'm rendered speechless. There's nothing more shocking to a 15-year-old boy than being revealed to himself in this way. I can't believe my mother so accurately described exactly what happened. I don't know what to do other than swear at her. "Fuck you," I shout. And that's just for starters. Now that the floodgates are opened, I launch into a stream of obscenity-laden vituperative that shocks me even now to think about it. Imagine the worst possible thing a male child can say to his female parent. What I say to my mother is even worse.

She just looks at me, absolutely aghast. Without a word, she gets up and leaves the room. I sit there, stewing in my own anger and embarrassment. Looking for something to blame, I kick the wig around a few times and toss it in the trash. I go to my room, slam the door, and turn up my music.

I'm still there when my father, having arrived home a little earlier, knocks and enters. He lifts the needle from the record player and gets my attention. "Your mother told me what you said to her this afternoon," he says.

"Oh great," I think. "Here we go. Here comes the lecture about how I ought to treat my mother with respect, how if it weren't for her, I'd never have been born, how I have to be a good son, blah-blah-blah."

But my dad takes a completely different approach. "David," he says to me, quite simply, but with a hard edge that I don't think I've ever really heard before. "Don't you ever talk to my wife that way again."

He pauses to let his words—and his gaze—bore into me. "Do you understand?"

I swallow hard. That's the best I can do.

"Good. Now, when you're ready to apologize to both of us, you can come down to dinner." And with that, he replaces the needle on my record and leaves, closing the door behind him.

For the second time today, I'm stunned by a parent. I have been fully expecting my father to guilt-trip me, to lay it on really thick about what a terrible son I am, to basically, talk down to me like I was some kind of idiot.

I mean, I know I've done an awful thing. I know what I said to my mom was completely out of line. I don't need to be told that my behavior was no way for a son to behave. And had my father taken that approach, I would have dismissed him altogether. I would have said to myself that my parents have such little respect for me that they won't even give me credit for knowing what's acceptable and what isn't. To state the obvious fact that my mother deserved an apology would have been patronizing. Even though I'm not officially an adult—and clearly, don't always behave like one—I want to be treated like one. When I'm reprimanded like a little child, I feel that my parents are failing to see who I am. And since, therefore, it's not really me they're reprimanding, I don't have to listen.

But my father didn't do any of that. By telling me that I had better not ever again talk to his wife that way, he was implicitly placing me on his level. He was treating me as an equal in this sense: he was reacting to my behavior as he would were he not my father and I not his son. He was talking to me man-to-man.

I feel scared. Impressed. And chastened. I feel as if I have been introduced into a whole new world, a world of adults who have relationships on equal footings. It is a world in which people have certain obligations to each other (one of which was not to say the sort of things I had said), but one in which those obligations are between men and women, not between parents and kids.

Although I don't feel very good about what I've done or about the prospect of apologizing to my mom, I feel proud of how my father has spoken to me. I feel that he's given me the respect I was implicitly asking for. I feel that he's treated me the way he would want me to treat him were the tables turned.

I wish I could say that I was therefore inspired to do the right thing—that I recognized the error of my ways and set out right there to make amends. I wish I could say I went straight downstairs and apologized to my mom. I don't, though. I stay in my room and stew for the rest of the evening.

The next morning, when I come down for breakfast, I pretend that nothing has happened. I pour myself a cup of coffee and heat up a Pop-Tart™ in the toaster. I can feel my parents' eyes on me as I slide into my seat at the breakfast table and pick up the sports page to read. Finally, I offer what amounts to the best I can do by way of apologizing at this point in my life.

"Mom," I say, with a slurp of my coffee. "You know, you were right about the wig. I was wrong so I guess I'm going to have to go get a haircut. Do you think you could take me?"

My mother, bless her heart, is willing to accept this as my way of saying I'm sorry. "Of course, you silly boy. Anything to keep those uptight bluenoses at your school from calling me again."

The incident thus recedes into the background as another minor family crisis to be overcome and forgotten. And though we do more or less sweep most of the details of the affair under the proverbial rug, I, for one, never forget the way both my parents treated me. The respect I was accorded (albeit undeserved) taught me a memorable lesson in how parents and children ought to behave towards one another. I will always remember how right it felt to be treated as I imagined I would have treated my own child. I only hope that in my ongoing tenure as a parent, I can do half as good a job of following the Golden Rule myself.

Golden Business

Comedian Emo Phillips tells a joke that describes how many businesspeople weigh their interests against the interests of their customers or co-workers.

"I found a wallet the other day," he says in his characteristic high-pitched whine, "with fifty dollars in it and an ID card of the person who lost it. And I said to myself, 'How would I feel if I lost my wallet with fifty dollars in it?' And the answer is: *I would want to be taught a lesson."*

The implication is obvious: Emo, having interpreted someone else's desires in the most self-interested manner possible, concludes that they must want what he wants: for Emo to keep the fifty bucks.

This is often how we think of our co-workers and customers. Instead of imagining what *they* really want, we imagine what we *want* them to want. Hardly the right way to understand and meet another person's needs. Hardly the right way to play fair.

Twentieth-century social and political philosopher John Rawls is famous for proposing a theory to ensure fairness in the rules by which society is governed. It is equally applicable as providing a principle by which our business dealings ought to be governed as well.

According to Rawls, rules that count as fair are those that everyone would agree to if everyone could freely and impartially choose them. Impartiality is guaranteed by having people choose those rules from behind what Rawls calls a "veil of ignorance." Think of the rules you would choose to be governed by if you didn't know anything about your own characteristics: your sex, age, race, class, etc. Presumably, to ensure that you didn't get the short end of the stick, you would try to make up rules that were as fair as possible to everyone, no matter what each person's particular characteristics were.

Warren Buffett, the billionaire entrepreneur and investor, did a nice job of explaining Rawls' theory in a speech he gave at the University of Washington. A student asked him how he would run things if he were in charge.

Let's say it's 24 hours before you're going to be born, and a genie appears. And the genie says, "You look like a real winner—I'm going to let you set the rules of society: economic, political, social.

And these rules are going to apply for your lifetime, and your children's lifetime, and grandchildren's."

So you ask, "What's the catch?"

The catch is, you don't know if you're going to be rich or poor, black or white, male or female . . . you have one ball among 5.8 billion in the ovarian lottery.

So what rules do you want to have?

We might ask ourselves a similar question with regard to the principles by which we would guide our behavior on the job. Suppose you didn't know whether you were your boss, your subordinate, your co-worker, your client, your supplier, a stockholder in your company, or a member of a community in which your company does business. From behind this "veil of ignorance," what principles would you choose to guide people's behavior? How would you sketch out possible scenarios so that no matter what character in that scenario you happened to be, the result for you would be as good as possible?

This way of thinking underpins the so-called "Stakeholder Theory" of corporate responsibility as originally conceived of by writers like Edward Freeman[8] and Charles Goodpaster.[9] According to the stakeholder theory of how businesses and businesspeople should act, a corporation's responsibilities go beyond merely maximizing profit. Executives need to recognize their obligations to six "stakeholder" groups, where a stakeholder is broadly defined as anyone who is affected by the corporation's activities. These groups are: customers, employees, suppliers, stockholders, management, and the local community.

There is much discussion in academic circles as to just what these responsibilities are and how they are to be dispatched. But several points bear repeating.

---

[8]See Freeman, R. Edward, "The Politics of Stakeholder Theory," *Business Ethics Quarterly,* 4 (1994), pp. 409–421.

[9]Goodpaster, Charles, "Business Ethics and Stakeholder Analysis," *Business Ethics Quarterly* 1 (January 1991), pp. 53–73.

First, as many writers—notably Tom Peters and Peter Drucker—have noted, there are good bottom-line reasons for companies to do right by their stakeholders. Companies that treat managers and employees well, that demonstrate respect for customers and suppliers, that contribute to the health of their communities, and that return a good value to stockholders will generally do better financially than companies that don't.

But not always. Sooner or later, nearly every business will encounter a situation in which it can maximize profits by *not* living up to its commitment to one or more stakeholders. On really hot days when people are dying of thirst, the kids with the corner lemonade stand can use one fewer lemon than advertised in their five-lemon lemonade formula, thereby saving on production costs, even though it means that customers get an inferior product. And since doing so won't hurt sales, what incentive is there to refrain from it?

By the same token, why should a major multinational corporation care about the effect on a local community's economy of closing down its factory if it can save money by moving operations somewhere else?

As long as businesses and businesspeople are motivated solely by bottom-line considerations, they will continue to experience this tension between fulfilling their obligations to stakeholders and maximizing profit.

It comes down to a question of motivation. For example, suppose the profitable thing to do *is* to treat stakeholders as they ought to be treated. Suppose as a businessperson, the reason I'm being fair to my employees, honest to my customers, and respectful to my community is because I realize it's profitable. But if so, am I really being just, fair, and respectful?

Many philosophers would say no. My reason for doing the right thing is all wrong. I'm making it a matter of self interest rather than of genuine concern for the welfare of others. I'm treating others as I would have me treat them, not as I would have them treat me.

Once again, we're back to the Golden Rule. We're back to identifying the right thing to do by exploring the needs of each party in the relationship. We're uncovering what our obligations are to others by examining how they perceive their responsibilities to us. We're holding a mirror up to the world so we can see ourselves— and ourselves seeing ourselves—on and on in an infinite sequence of reflections.

But as Norman Bowie has pointed out, this means that the relationships among businesses and their stakeholders have to be a two-way street.[10] If, as employees, we expect our employers to treat us with dignity and respect, we need to fulfill our obligations to be loyal and trustworthy. Or if, as customers, we want businesses to "go the extra mile" for us, it's only fair that we be willing to do the same for them.

The idea that there are what Bowie calls "reciprocal obligations" among a business' stakeholders was brought home to me recently as I pondered the right thing to do in a little transaction with one of my favorite local businesses.

My neighborhood bicycle shop is your classic local bike shop (LBS). They have a large, somewhat eclectic selection of bicycles and a bustling repair facility that services everything from custom-made high-end racing cycles to cheap mass-produced kids' bikes. I have been a customer of this LBS ever since I moved to Seattle, and I have established a pretty good relationship with John, the repair shop manager.

John has helped me out a number of times with various fixes to my small collection of bicycles, giving me loads of free advice, assistance, and moral support. One time, for instance, I'd managed to completely freeze the bolt that connects my left pedal to its crankarm. I was prepared to buy a new set of cranks (around $60.00) to remedy the situation. John simply put the crank in a vice, and using a large wrench

---

[10]Bowie, Norman, "New Directions in Corporate Social Responsibility," *Business Horizons* 34 (July/August 1991), pp. 56–65.

and a pipe as a "cheater bar," easily turned the pedal free. On another occasion, when I was thinking of buying a new gear cassette (at least $40.00) to extend the range of my lowest gear, he dug around in a box of parts and gave me the one large cog I really needed for free.

Best of all, though, John doesn't make me feel like an idiot when I come in and ask questions. Unlike mechanics in many bike shops, he's supportive of home tinkerers like me. I'm not afraid to ask him for the third time which way the bottom bracket cup spins off on the bike's left side. I don't get the rolled eyes that most bike repairers give me when I accidentally call a "chain ring" a "cog," or vice versa.

Because of this, I continue to be a loyal customer of my LBS. Even though it's a bit out of the way for me and even though some items are less expensive elsewhere, I generally shop there for all my cycling needs.

Now, however, I'm faced with a slight quandary. I think I need a new rear derailleur—the component that moves the chain from cog to cog when you shift gears. I'd been having a little trouble with my current one; and my efforts to repair it have unfortunately—but not without precedent—only exacerbated the problem.

I took it into the LBS the other day, entirely prepared to have to buy a new one. John looked at it and showed me what was wrong: the so-called "breakaway bolt" that affixes it to the bike's frame was rusted. He showed me how to take the derailleur apart to get at it. "Just run a bunch of lube in there," he said, "and pop the bolt out with a mallet. Then lube it all back up and put it back in. Should be good as new."

I've taken his advice, and even though it wasn't quite as simple as all that (it took me a hammer and a pair of channel-locks to get the bolt out), I've managed to get the component back together and put it back on my bike. Unfortunately, even though the breakaway bolt now flexes as easily as it's supposed to, the derailleur still doesn't shift well. I apparently bent it trying to get the bolt out. So now, whenever I shift onto the cogs closest to the wheel, the chain rubs against the derailleur cage and slips out of gear.

I call the LBS to get a price on a new derailleur. John isn't there, but Scott, another of the mechanics, gives me a quote of $60.00 for the model I need.

I hang up, kind of shocked. Poking around recently on the website for one of the big mail-order places, I've seen the same derailleur on sale for $29.99.

What am I to do? I recognize that I have some obligation to my LBS, a duty of gratitude for all the free help they've given me, but thirty bucks is thirty bucks. We're talking about a 100% higher price for the same component. Does my obligation extend that far?

I try to put myself in my LBS's shoes, specifically, John's. If I were him, how would I feel knowing that, in spite of our ongoing relationship, my customer bailed on me just to get a lower price from a company that, quite frankly, we can't possibly compete with on cost alone? The answer is obvious: I'd feel lousy. Betrayed. Taken advantage of.

This suggests that indeed there are reciprocal obligations between businesses and customers. By opting to buy from the mail-order house, I'm clearly shirking those obligations.

Obviously, this isn't the answer I'm hoping for. I want some justification for buying mail order. I want it to come out so that purchasing at the lower price is the right thing to do.

I decide to share my dilemma with the business ethics class I'm teaching. My students are mostly 19- and 20-year-olds. I'm pretty sure I can count on them to support me in making the purely self-interested choice.

They let me down, though. Surprisingly, the vast majority of them insist that because my LBS has consistently given me free service, I have a responsibility to pay them back in kind.

"They have a right to be treated as they treat you," says Mike, a psychology major, who usually sits in front and always keeps me on my toes.

"But thirty bucks is a lot of money," I argue feebly.

"Hey. You're the one who told us about stakeholder theory and reciprocal obligations," answers Mike. "If you don't like what it implies, you should have taught us something else."

Mike's right, of course. If I am honestly going to abide by the underlying principle of the Golden Rule, then the relationship between businesses and customers has to be conceived of as a two-way street. There's no denying it. The right thing to do is buy the derailleur from my LBS, even though it's more expensive there.

After class, I ride my bike to the bikeshop, gingerly nursing my balky gear. I've resolved to purchase the new derailleur from my LBS, but I'm hoping that if I explain the situation to John, maybe he'll give me a break on the price. (It seems to me that it's not inconsistent with the Golden Rule to ask for a discount. I figure that if I were John, I wouldn't mind the request. Granted, I might not fill it, but that's another matter—and one that, as his customer, I'm prepared to live with if I have to.)

I wheel my bike through the door of the shop and spy John.

"What's up?" he asks as I approach the repair area.

I'm all prepared to launch into my explanation of the problem and my well-rehearsed plea for a discount.

"I think I need that new derailleur after all," I begin.

John leans over and looks at my bike. "It's hitting the spokes, huh?"

"Yes, and I was wondering if you'd be willing to consider—"

John stops me before I can get my request out.

"Hold on." He steps behind the repair counter and returns with a comically huge pipe wrench.

My story now has a happy ending.

John grabs my derailleur in the jaws of the wrench and gives a mighty twist. "That oughtta do it," he says.

And it has. By bending the metal back into place, John has fixed my bike as good as new—without having to purchase a thing. He's saved me more than merely the difference in price between the mail-order price and the LBS'; he's saved me from having to spend anything at all.

The least I can do is buy him a six-pack of beer. It's a quick ride to the store and back with my bike running so well.

Sometimes, we get lucky like that. Sometimes it turns out that the right thing to do is completely within our self-interest. We get what we want by doing what we should. In such cases, then, we have every reason for doing the right thing. It's easy to convince ourselves to make the moral choice.

But it doesn't always work that way. Lots of times, doing the right thing feels pretty unnatural. It seems as if our nature is at conflict with morality. Nature, it appears, tells us to maximize our own interests; morality apparently tells us to place the needs of others on a par with our own.

But does this tension really exist? Is morality really at war with nature? Or is there another way of looking at our relationship to the natural world that makes doing the right thing less of a struggle? If the answers to these questions interests you, then the perfectly natural thing to do is turn to Chapter 5, "Right in Place."

Chapter Five

Right in Place

Doing Right by the Planet

Doing What Mother Nature Says

In every introductory ethics class, there are always a few students who want to argue that morality is nothing more than a way to ensure the survival of the human species. Our conceptions of right and wrong, they say, are entirely a by-product of evolution; the real reason we think something is good is because it contributes to the passing down of our genetic material to future generations; the real reason we say it's bad is because it reduces the likelihood of having descendants.

There's certainly something to be said for this view. If the right thing to do consistently resulted in our inability to procreate, we probably wouldn't keep thinking it was the right thing to do. We're not lemmings, after all—contrary to the impressions of many politicians and advertising executives.

On the other hand, it's hard to accept that right and wrong are *entirely* the result of natural selection. If that were the case, then it would be much harder to explain why rape or adultery, for instance, are generally—and quite justifiably—considered to be wrong.

But there must be some connection between what's natural and what's right. We're not lemmings, that's for sure, but we *are* animals. And as animals, we're at least partly determined by nature. So, while nature may not be the *only* arbiter of right and wrong, it must have an important vote. And indeed, many enlightened observers of humankind, from Aristotle to Emerson, from Henry David Thoreau to Wendell Berry, have reminded us that nature provides us with critical guidance when it comes to figuring out what we ought to do.

How then, does this relate to the moral spectrum model? How does the obvious connection between what's natural and what's right inform our ability to perceive and choose the right thing to do? Perhaps the following example will provide some insight.

Sixth grade, and Jeffrey Goldberg is one of my heroes. Supersmart, funny, great athlete, he is definitely the star of Mrs. Ferrante's homeroom class. I'm not really Jeff's friend—nor, to tell the truth, is anyone; his greatness somehow distances him from us mere mortals—but, like everyone, I am friendly with him. You would have to be crazy not to be nice to the guy; it would be like being mean to the Pope or something.

One day, though, something gets into me. Maybe it is the two boxes of Jujubees and three cans of Orange Crush I had for lunch. But I somehow, I find myself attacking Jeff on the schoolbus. I think I am egged on by my ubiquitous torturer, Charles Titterington. I seem to recall that Charles gives me the option of either fighting him or Jeff. Discretion being in my case the *only* part of valor, I opt for sucker-punching an unsuspecting nice guy rather than getting pummeled by a fully-prepared bully.

Surprisingly, but true to his amiable nature, Jeff doesn't turn around and clobber me. He simply swivels about in his seat and gives me a withering look of shock and disappointment.

Charles interprets it for me. "He's gonna kick your ass, Shapiro. You'd better run when we get off the bus."

I don't wait around when we get to school to find out if Charles has correctly read Jeff's mood. No sooner does the busdriver open the door than I am sprinting past my classmates towards the safety of my home.

I burst in the front door and announce to my mom that we have to go to the toy store to buy a present for Jeff Goldberg. She wants to know why. I explain that Jeff is a really great guy and that I want to do something nice for him. Besides, it is his birthday and we are having a party for him in class. Plus, we drew to see who ought to pick up his gift and I was chosen.

My natural instinct for survival is functioning in high gear. I have no qualms about cowardice, dishonesty, or bribery as a means to save my sorry hide.

My mother happens to be on her way to the mall anyway, so agrees to drop me off at the toy store. I finagle ten bucks out of her on the pretense that we're taking up a collection in class and the promise that I'll pay her back as soon as everyone contributes, thus adding petty thievery to my repertoire of hide-saving strategies.

I pick out a copy of "All-Star Baseball" for Jeff, a board game that is all the rage at the time. It's my favorite pastime and I flatter myself to think that Jeff will love it too. I even have visions of playing it with him— and nice guy that I am, I'll be sure and let him win the first few times.

The next morning, I get to school early and slip the game into Jeff's locker. Instead of attaching a note to his gift, I hang out down the hall behind the fire extinguisher to see him discover it. When he opens his locker, the game falls out. With his quick hands, he catches it easily.

I saunter up, somewhat warily (but fairly sure Jeff won't attack me inside the school building and probably not while his hands are full of "All-Star Baseball), and say, "Jeff. Hi. Howdya like the game?"

He looks me up and down and turns the package over but doesn't say a word. I try to fill the empty conversational space.

"I thought you'd like it. It's really cool. Maybe we could play sometimes."

Jeff furrows his brow and looks at me. He cocks his head as if trying to pour my words through his brain so they'll make sense. After a moment he asks, "You're giving me this game?"

"Well yeah," I shrug. "I just wanted you to have it and you know . . . it's a cool game."

Jeff sighs. He shakes his head with a world-weariness that belies his tender age. "Whatever," he says. "Thanks, I guess. But I can't accept this." He holds the game out for me to take.

Feeling confident that I have avoided a beating, I press my luck. "No, keep it. Really. Why don't we play after school? You could come over to my house. I'll show you the rules and how to make a really good team."

"I don't think so," says Jeff. "In fact, I sorta wish you'd leave me alone."

Jeff easily reads the question on my face. "I'm not gonna beat you up or anything for yesterday," he says. "Just don't try to be my friend, okay?" And with that, he drops the game on the floor and departs for class.

Charles Titterington suddenly appears from the stairwell where he's been watching the whole thing. "Shapiro, you wuss! I can't believe you tried to buy Goldberg off with a bribe! Man, you are pathetic."

"I didn't try to buy him off," I lie. "I just wanted him to have it. What's wrong with that?"

"I oughtta kick your ass right now for being such a sleazeball," growls Charles, grabbing my shirt.

"No. No," I stammer. "Here," I said, reaching down to pick up the unopened copy of "All-Star Baseball" at the foot of Jeff's locker. "You can have it. If Jeff doesn't want it, it's yours."

Charles releases me to take the game. "Cool. All right, but if I hear about some sissy-assed trick like this again, your ass is grass, got it?"

I nod. Charles gives me a friendly little slap on the cheek, just hard enough to make tears spring to my eyes. "And don't think just because Goldberg didn't whup you that you're Mr. Cool. Just because he's letting you live doesn't mean you're not a jagoff." And with that, he shoves me against Jeff's locker and strolls away, tearing the shrink-wrap off of his prize.

Charles' own morals—and motives—may have been suspect, but his assessment of mine were absolutely right on. Just because my behavior toward Jeff contributed to my "survival,"[11] wasn't enough to make it right. My guilt over the unprovoked attack was perfectly natural. And it certainly made sense to express my penitence via a gift of some sort. Sociobiologists and evolutionary philosophers could easily explain my behavior in terms of natural selection: individuals who, like me, attempt to defuse the anger of others by expressing remorse and offering resources are more likely to see their genetic material passed down to future generations. Therefore, there's an evolutionary advantage to guilt and penitence; that's why we judge them to be the appropriate response in situations like the one I found myself in with Jeff.

But as Charles pointed out, their appropriateness alone—even their purported evolutionary advantage—doesn't make them the right thing to do. There has to be something more than mere genetic expediency to make something morally acceptable. Certainly, in my case, cowardice, dishonesty, bribery, and thievery weren't justified simply because they saved my butt.

On the other hand, my *actions* towards Jeff weren't so bad. You can't completely reproach me for trying to make amends—in spite of how clumsy and self-serving my attempt was. Apologizing, and perhaps even compensating him in some way for my attack, was

---

[11] I mean that in a general sense of "survival"; since this was before the days of so many guns in the hands of schoolkids, Jeff wouldn't *really* have killed me.

indeed called for. So my natural instincts at least pointed me in the right direction, even if they weren't enough to establish the virtuousness of my behavior.

Many people—Immanuel Kant, for one—would say that what I was lacking was the proper motive. Since my apology to Jeff wasn't motivated by a sense of moral duty, my behavior doesn't qualify as moral either. Kant would complain that I wasn't acting out of a sense of moral duty; since my motivation was self-preservation, rather than a proper recognition of my duty to apologize, my action had no authentic moral worth.

This may at first seem like a pretty stringent requirement, but in fact, it does jibe pretty well with our usual way of looking at things. We *do* judge people differently depending on their motives. Our assessment of someone who risks his life to capture a criminal in hopes of earning a big reward is different than our judgment of someone who does so because she recognizes it's her duty to do so. Bounty hunters don't earn our praise; dedicated law enforcement officials do.

But why should it matter? What difference does it make whether someone is motivated by money or by duty? Or for that matter, by self-preservation or morality? A captured criminal is a captured criminal, right? An apology is an apology, isn't it?

Well, for one thing, the proper motivation makes a difference in how abiding someone's commitment to doing the right thing is going to be. If people do the right thing for the right reasons, they're more apt to do so consistently. If it's only because they desire praise or fear punishment, then in the absence of those incentives, they'll be less likely to make the right choice. We've all seen this with kids on a schoolyard. You break up their fight and make them shake hands. Begrudgingly, and only because you threaten to haul them off to the principal if they don't, they reach out and touch fingers. No sooner do you stroll away, feeling proud of yourself for fostering peace in the world than the two assailants are back at it, rubbing each other's faces in the dirt.

The question then is: How do we develop the proper motivation? How do we come to do the right thing for the right reasons—and not just because we'll be punished or beaten up if we don't?

One answer is to examine the situation through a number of different moral prisms. We can ask ourselves the seven questions that constitute the moral spectrum model:

E "What course(s) of action will set people most free?"

D "What would I do if everyone in the world were to do as I did?"

C "What course(s) of action will best sustain and nurture a caring relationship between myself and others?"

C "How would I act if everyone in my community knew exactly what I were doing?"

U "What course(s) of action will best maximize total happiness in the world?"

V "What would the most virtuous person I know of do in this situation?"

E "What course(s) of action will most effectively ensure that my short- and long-term goals are reached?"

Had I the wherewithal to query myself in this way before buying Jeff his game, I might have approached things differently. Certainly, I would have been embarrassed to have all my friends and family know that I was trying to buy Jeff's good will. And although—assuming Jeff did like the game—*his* happiness may have increased, it's a safe bet that my mom's pleasure would have been diminished by my lying to her. Moreover, I seriously doubt whether anyone would want to live in a world where people so blatantly sucked up to each other in the interest of self-preservation. The fullest expression of human freedom may have been to buy Jeff the game, but then again, that would be attempting to stifle his free judgment of my behavior. My short-term goal of not getting beaten up would indeed be met, but my longer-term goal of being admired by Jeff would be seriously compromised by such weasly behavior. This would also undermine any care Jeff felt toward me. But perhaps most tellingly of all, the person I considered most virtuous in the world—Jeff Goldberg himself—would never have acted the way I did.

So here's a clear case in which the right thing to do is not completely captured by the natural thing to do. There's plenty of overlap, but that's what makes it confusing. If we try to rely solely on what our genes say we ought to do, we may come close to making good choices, but we'll also regularly stumble. And even if we do happen to behave in the right way, it's not entirely likely that we'll be doing so for the right reasons. Consequently, we'll be inconsistent in our behavior at best, and merely self-serving and selfish at worst.

Nature: Moral or Immoral?

If it's true that nature provides us with *some* moral guidance but isn't in itself sufficient to justify our determinations of right and wrong, then what role should it play in our thinking? Some writers have argued that moral development consists in our overcoming the demands of our animal natures. Biologist Richard Dawkins famously refers to our genes as "selfish"[12] and argues that behaving morally is a matter of—in the broadest sense—rebelling against the tyranny of these selfish replicators.[13] This view is echoed by ethicist Peter Singer, who urges us to learn much as possible about genetics so we can get beyond our biological tendencies toward aggression and selfishness in order to develop higher standards of morality which we can pass down to future generations.[14] And it is presaged by Charles Darwin's student Thomas Huxley, who, at the turn of

---

[12]Dawkins, Richard, *The Selfish Gene* (Oxford: Oxford University Press), book title.

[13]ibid., p 215.

[14]Singer, Peter, *The Expanding Circle* (Reader, pp. 215–216).

this century, wrote "Let us understand, once for all, that the ethical progress of society depends, not on imitating the cosmic process, still less on running away from it, but in combating it."[15] But Dawkins' position finds perhaps its most ardent supporter in the contemporary sociobiologist George C. Williams, who contends that Huxley, for one, didn't go far enough in his condemnation of evolution as a determinant of the right thing to do. According to Williams, natural selection may be worse than warfare,[16] so much so that "The conscience of man must revolt against the gross immorality of nature."[17]

Contrary to Dawkins (and especially Williams) are numerous philosophers, sociobiologists, and economists[18] who argue in one way or another that what we usually think of as moral behavior—say, altruism—can be explained biologically. R. J. Richards, for example, argues that a moral sense has evolved in human beings and that, consequently, an ethics based on presumed facts about biological evolution can be justified by those facts.[19] Robert Frank purports to explain, in biological terms, how the moral emotions have developed; he describes how feelings of generosity, love, and, indeed, authentically altruistic behavior could have arisen in human beings as part of our ongoing evolutionary development. But perhaps no one is more sympathetic to this sort of naturalistic explanation of human morality than sociobiologists John Collier and Michael Stingl, who argue that not only is morality determined by

---

[15]Huxley, Thomas H., *Evolution and Ethics and Other Essays* (New York: D. Appleton, 1894), quoted in Williams, George C., "Huxley's Evolution and Ethics in Sociobiological Perspective," in Thompson, Paul (Ed.), *Issues in Evolutionary Ethics* (Albany: State University of NY Press, 1995), p. 317.

[16]Williams, George C., "Huxley's Evolution and Ethics in Sociobiological Perspective," in Thompson, Paul (Ed.), *Issues in Evolutionary Ethics* (Albany: State University of NY Press, 1995), p. 318.

[17]ibid., p. 319.

[18]Here I have in mind, for instance, Michael Ruse, R. J. Richards, and Robert Frank.

[19]Richards, R. J., "A Defense of Evolutionary Ethics," in Thompson, p. 258.

general facts of evolution as applied to creatures such as us[20], but, furthermore, evolution seems to be guiding us, albeit by fits and starts, toward an optimal morality. We may, for any number of reasons, not get there, but Collier and Stingl are least confident that the evolution of morality is made likely by evolution.[21]

Such divergent positions on the relationship between evolution and morality are evidence of a fascinating dialectic at work, as researchers and theorists from a variety of disciplines attempt to uncover the origins of human morality. But they are also evidence, I think, of problems associated with putting too much stock in evolution as either the cause of or the foil for our ethical beliefs and behaviors. Both sides, in either demonizing or canonizing natural selection, raise difficulties that seem to run counter to our standard notions of what morality entails. By so wholeheartedly either embracing or rejecting evolution, both views paint themselves into corners that are cut off from essential features of a full-fledged morality.

Perhaps a middle position is the right way to think about things. This middle position would suppose that morality is a matter of both fighting against and working with evolution. It would imagine that there are some instances in which our genes incline us in a moral direction, others in which they lead us astray. Here we might begin to carve out a position that embraces the benefits of both sides of the debate.

Of course, filling out this position would require quite a bit of work. For one thing, we would have to figure out *when* to work with evolution and when to fight against it. This would require that we *first* develop some sort of independent criteria for morality, which unfortunately is just what we're trying to end up with. For another, we would have to develop a theory of how to go about criticizing evolution. But, since presumably our critical tools have

---

[20]Collier, John, and Michael Stingl, "Evolutionary Naturalism and the Objectivity of Morality," in Thompson, p. 426.

[21]ibid.

been supplied by evolution, it's an open question whether or not they are too tainted by their development to be of independent critical use.

Ultimately, in order to develop moral principles from the pressures of natural selection, we need to be able examine the attitudes, beliefs, and behaviors that follow from our genetic tendencies and pass judgment on them. We need to be able to say, for instance, that the natural sympathies parents feel for their children (which have obviously been selected for) is a good thing, while the antipathy that different ethnic groups often manifest toward each other (which probably has a biological story behind it as well) is not. And this is going to require that we have the ability to critique our naturally selected-for tendencies from an independent vantage point.

Finding that independent vantage point promises to be difficult, but it's not impossible. We have precedents in medicine, for instance, which has established independent criteria for health. It's not a matter of opinion whether extremely high blood pressure is worse than normal blood pressure—for anyone who's interested in living a long and healthful life, it *is* worse. So perhaps it's just a matter of thinking about nature in a slightly different way.

Nature as Oracle

If nature isn't our infallible guide, perhaps we can conceive of it as an oracle.

Oracles are different than guides; they're less literal, more impressionistic. Unlike guides, which tell us exactly where to go, oracles merely provide hints, letting us figure things out for ourselves. Oracles can be puzzling; they often speak in riddles. We have to decipher their messages and make sense of them in context of our own lives. But because of this, oracles focus our thinking. Since we have to ponder an oracle's message, we are compelled to introspect, and in doing so, can discover knowledge we weren't aware we had. Making sense of what an oracle tells us is often a matter of coming to a clearer understanding of what we knew vaguely all along.

Famous oracles include the Oracle at Delphi, through which the God Apollo supposedly spoke, dispatching wisdom to well-known ancients like Socrates and Oedipus, or the Oracle at Dodana, where Zeus was thought to answer through the rustling of oak leaves. Typically, the Delphic Oracle's message to Socrates was mysterious, paradoxically suggesting the he was the wisest of all Athenians because he alone knew he knew nothing.

In our own day and age, the oracles we consult include everything from stock market analysts to television meteorologists. Or we use our daily horoscope or a fortune cookie fortune to help us decide. A flipped coin is an oracle many of us consult quite regularly: no sooner do we uncover the coin and what it tells us to do than we decide we prefer the alternative.

Treating nature as an oracle is different from blindly following its dictates—that is, doing "what's natural." Rather, it's about authentically seeing the natural world's message and interpreting it wisely. Nature is not our master here; it is our trusted consultant. But even so, it is a somewhat capricious advisor. Its advice is open to interpretation. To understand its wisdom, we must be sufficiently wise ourselves.

So how do we come to this wisdom? How do we develop the ability to correctly interpret nature's message?

One way to approach this challenge is to develop a perspective on things as richly varied as nature herself. We can explore the inherent complexity of the situations we face in our lives with an approach that seeks to mirror this fullness. Were we exploring nature, we would improve our understanding by examining it from as many angles and perspectives as possible. We would take the long view; we would hone in microscopically; we would look at things from above, below, and the side; we would engage all our senses in our effort to understand; and we would conduct our study with an appreciation of the ever-changing nature of our subject. In short, we would recognize that we could never hope to grasp the richness of nature unless we employed means that were equally rich.

It makes sense to approach complex questions of right and

wrong in our own lives with a similar willingness to explore. Instead of always trying to simplify the issues in order to make sense of them, perhaps we may do better to—at least occasionally—complicate them. Rather than sorting through the data and discarding anything that runs counter to a judgment we are intent upon defending, maybe we can try embracing all the information that presents itself and allow ourselves to discover where it leads.

How might this look?

Consider the sort of question—about nature, as a matter of fact—that is so prevalent in my neck of the woods nowadays: How ought we to manage our shared natural resources, in particular, stands of old-growth timber? Loggers and environmentalists line up on either side of the debate, the former arguing that the potential loss of people's jobs outweighs the potential loss of animal habitats, the latter charging that the intrinsic rights of nature trump the economic freedom of corporations and employees. The discourse takes place with all the dignity of a television talk show, as both parties trade bumper sticker slogans like, "Spotted Owl Stew Served Here," and "Loggers Suck."

Would it make any difference if the disputants—instead of trying to *enlist* nature as an ally in support their positions—*appealed* to nature as an oracle to broaden their perspectives? Would there be room for accommodation between their views if they examined the situation through more than one moral prism?

We can assume that the pro-logging camp takes a utilitarian perspective on the issue. Their position is buttressed by economic arguments that rely on the satisfaction of people's preferences to have relatively high-paying jobs and steady paychecks.

The pro-environment camp can be seen as appealing to a deontological perspective, one that asks what would happen if everyone behaved as the logging companies do. Assuming that this would result in the absence of forests everywhere, it then concludes that such behavior is not the right thing to do.

Both sides are pretty well dug into their positions; after years and years of trading barbs, neither is much inclined to entertain the other side's point of view. But suppose both were willing to broaden their horizons by trying out another moral prism. Isn't it possible that a new way of looking at things might result in an openness to some sort of compromise?

According to the moral spectrum model, utilitarians—who are focused on principles, outcomes, and society—and deontologists—whose attention is turned to principles, motives, and individuals—can find common ground by exploring shared principles. But what would such principles be? Given the chasm that separates the two sides, it's hard to imagine that there is any underlying theme upon which both could agree.

Here, though, is where the idea of nature as oracle can come in. By exploring what principle nature might be offering as its oracular message, both sides could conceivably move closer together. Of course, it's going to be quite difficult to say what this principle is. *Survival of the fittest? Diversity equals strength? Everything is one?* But even so, the very possibility of nature revealing such a principle opens up room for dialogue and mutual exploration. No longer would both parties necessarily be at each other's throat. Instead of fighting against one another, they'd be engaged in a process of shared investigation. Of course, this wouldn't guarantee that there'd be no conflict, but it would at least provide a framework for agreement and a means to begin a solution-oriented dialogue.

Nature as God

Seventeenth-century philosopher Benedict Spinoza is famous—or infamous—for denying a separation between God and nature. For Spinoza, everything that exists is ultimately an attribute of God; there can be, therefore, no distinction between the Creator and the creation. Essentially, nature *is* God, and vice versa. Moreover, our minds and our bodies are one and the same thing, expressed in two ways, so when you get right down to it, the highest good we can experience is the knowledge of the oneness of our minds with the whole of nature.

Because of his theological perspective, Spinoza is often labeled a *pantheist*—someone who believes in many gods. But perhaps a better way to characterize him is as an *omnitheist*—someone who believes that God is everywhere. Our salvation as human beings consists in the loving union of our consciousness with God—that is, nature. And since, as Spinoza observes, all happiness or unhappiness we feel is tied to the quality of the object to which we cling with love, true happiness will result only from loving that which is eternal—in other words, from loving all of nature. Not that this will be easy; as Spinoza reminds us, all things excellent are as difficult as they are rare. Still, with effort, the peace of mind that comes from achieving mental union with nature can be achieved. It follows upon the recognition that the more the mind enjoys the blessedness of loving nature, the greater its power to avoid evil and embrace the good. Here, nature as oracle resides within and all about us; we come to our true fullness of being by recognizing this and loving nature unconditionally.

This might sound pretty far beyond the way we can ever hope to experience the world. But not so. Most of us have, at one time or another, experienced that feeling of being entirely at one with the universe in a way that fits Spinoza's description of a blessed love. Such instances are rare, but they are deeply memorable. Nor do they require us to have come from any particular religious background or participated in any special kind of spiritual training. Even children can have such experiences, as I hope the following anecdote attests to.

As a rambunctious boy of 8, I am the proverbial handful—a bossy, impatient, temper-tantrum throwing handful, to be more precise. A typical day begins with me destroying the kitchen in my haste to consume a bowl of Cocoa Puffs, proceeds through an equally calamitous exploration of my parents' record collection, detours into a explosive expression of my desire to be taken to the local hobby shop/slot car racing store, and all this before it is time to leave for school. Summertime then, is a special delight for my parents, as I have all day to get into trouble and complain about my inability to get into more. Every few hours or so, I throw myself down on whatever piece of furniture is handy and announce in no uncertain terms that I am bored, that there is nothing to do, and that the only possible solution to this is for my parents to run right out and buy me a brand-new minibike.

My mother's typical response is to suggest quite reasonably—but with tongue firmly implanted in cheek—that if I am so terribly bored, why don't I just go get lost in the woods? Normally, I respond by complaining about the injustice of having been born so far from the seashore or a drag-racing track, but on this day, I decide to take her up on it.

The woods behind our house are no Amazon jungle; they're just a bunch of trees separating a number of emerging suburban subdivisions. But to my 8-year-old perspective, they appear as dense and dark as the Montana wilderness. Usually, I stick to familiar paths that wind through from one backyard to another. Today, though, when I venture in, I stray, cautiously at first, but then with a bit more abandon.

About the time I think I might want begin heading back, I hear the gruff bark of what sounds like two very large dogs. Fearing attack by the wild Doberman "Pinchers" that are rumored among my friends to eat neighborhood children, I plunge into the trees. Branches whip my face as I stumble forward, away from the angry growling. By the time I have put the sound behind me, I am deep into the brush—totally soaked in sweat, and completely lost.

I try retracing my steps, but it's hopeless. Hidden by the underbrush, the paths are unidentifiable. Nothing looks familiar. I come upon a rock that I think I recognize, but when I strike out from it toward where I believe home is, I soon find myself having circled back upon it, no closer to my destination at all.

In short order, I become frantic. I begin running blindly through the woods, almost as if it is pursuing me, in an attempt to make my house appear. Tears stream down my face and I breathe in great, heaving sobs. I simultaneously curse my mom for letting me get lost and beseech her to come find me.

Then, up ahead, I spy a clearing. I break for it, assured that my backyard is only moments away. But when I stagger from the trees into the tall grass, my elation turns to horror. This isn't my backyard; this isn't any place in the world I've ever seen before. Moreover, I must be literally miles from home, for up in front of me stands something even more frightening than the feared "Pinchers": horses! Three brown mares are grazing in the field not twenty feet away. Two of them look up and I freeze in my tracks.

I feel a wail rising in my throat. The ground begins to spin. At that moment though, something very strange begins to happen, something that is both utterly foreign but entirely familiar.

I suddenly feel as if I am standing on the very top of the world—I am the world's pole and it is turning beneath me, rotating just under my feet. At the same time, my arms seem to rise into the sky such that I am extended like a great contrail across the horizon. I seem to be observing this from afar, as if I am poring over an image in the world's largest picture book. I feel as if I can turn the page and make anything happen that I want. Instead, I remain enraptured by this tableau and let myself experience the moment as fully as possible.

I don't feel 8 years old anymore; I don't feel any age. Even now, when I think back on it , I don't see myself as a child in that moment. In fact, whoever it was having that experience was far older and wiser than I am right now.

The boundaries that separate us from the world-at-large seem to fall away. I stand not within nature, nor upon it, but as part of it. I can hear the hum of blueflies in the field, the swish of the grass as the wind blows upon it, the chuckle of the horses as they eat, but these sounds flow directly through me. My overriding sense is of being a single cell within the total body of nature. The blood that courses through my veins is pumped by nature's heart, the air that I breathe fills nature's lungs, too. The image that remains of this moment is of my body, back-lit by the late afternoon sun, just one shape in the totality of nature's puzzle. I am a tree, a cloud, a single blade of grass waving gently in the summer breeze.

And in that moment, I know exactly what to do: nothing. That is, in standing there, a part of nature—not apart from it—I am doing everything I need to do. My fear falls away. I am no longer lost. I am as at home in my surroundings as the blueflies, the grass, and the horses.

After an eternity that, in fact, lasts no more than a minute or two, I make my way through the field to a farmhouse that stands at its far end. The house is the last remaining holdout to the inevitable suburbanization around it, and its owners are straight out of central casting for the cantankerous, but kindly, old farm couple who aren't gonna sell. The farmer sits me down at his kitchen table and calls my mom. His wife gives me a piece of pie and a glass of milk.

When my mother arrives to drive me home, she and the couple have a good laugh over the idea that I have taken literally her suggestion to get lost in the woods. In the car on the way home, she speaks to me more seriously.

"Please don't do that again, David. You gave me quite a scare."

I nod.

"But you did the right thing by not panicking and going to that house for help. How did you know?"

I shrug my shoulders. "I don't know, Mom. I just did what seemed natural. I listened to the horses and the grass in the field. They told me. The sky and the trees told me. It wasn't my decision. It was everything around me that showed me where to go."

She takes her eyes off the road for a second to look at me. I smile a crooked smile. She shakes her head and sighs. But when she laughs softly as she returns her gaze to the road, I believe she knows what I mean.

And I think we all do, at some level, know what that 8-year-old boy was talking about. While we don't regularly experience that oneness with nature so dramatically, it's not an entirely uncommon occurrence. It may happen at any time, in any surrounding, alone or with a group of people. But most of us are familiar with the feeling of connection that occasionally occurs, a feeling in which the universe seems to be speaking through us in a very direct and meaningful way. And when it does, we seem to know exactly what we ought to do, even if we're in a situation we've never encountered before. The right choice presents itself as the obvious choice. As a matter of fact, it's hardly a "choice" at all; it's simply the right thing to do.

Presumably, our development as wise human beings can be in part a matter of developing a closer, more consistent connection to this feeling. But how do we do that? How do we attune our sensibilities to the messages around us? How do we figure out what nature wants?

Nature as Self

Opening oneself to what Spinoza called the "knowledge of the union that the mind has with the whole of nature" is a matter of opening oneself to a particular kind of knowledge. And assuming, as we have been, that right and wrong are real properties of the natural world—albeit properties that are intimately connected to our emotional responses—then this knowledge is expanded by enhancing our ability to perceive the right thing to do. The promise of the moral spectrum model is that it helps us improve our perception of what's right and so, by extension, our access to the union we seek. Whether it succeeds or not is an open question, but one that may be best discovered through practice rather than mere discussion.

The particulars of that practice seem to be a matter of individual choice. There's no reason, for instance, we'd want to advocate a single way for people to *be* in coming to a better understanding of right and wrong. As a matter of fact, we ought to be skeptical of a program that stipulates exactly how one should behave in all situations. The diversity of nature itself should remind us that there is an infinite number of viable lifestyle options. An unmarried, urban-dwelling, street musician ought to have equal opportunity to live a moral life as does a farmer with three kids living in the country.

What does seem critical, though, is the recognition of one's place in the universe, a sense of participation in a larger context.

It's hard to see how someone can appreciate that their choices really do make a difference—either positively or negatively—unless those choices are understood within the framework of a wider context. Moreover, unless that context has some independent—that is to say, *natural*—standing, then people may be less likely to take seriously the reality of those positive or negative effects. For this reason, seeing our lives as part of the temporal and spatial fabric of nature seems to play an important part in our ability to perceive and choose the right thing to do.

The good news, though, is that this sort of broad perspective tends to be something toward which we naturally gravitate in our ongoing search for happiness. A fulfilling human life may indeed require just the sort of appreciation for nature and natural processes upon which wise moral choices are predicated.

Eco-philosopher Robert Goodin touches on this idea in his book *Green Political Theory*. According to Goodin, the source of our valuing the natural world follows from three characteristics of human beings. First, we want to see some sense and pattern to our lives. Second, this requires that we set our lives in some larger context. And third, for beings such as us, the products of natural processes provide that desired context.[22]

We are, of course, entitled to wonder what exactly qualifies as a product of a natural process and especially about whether or not human artifacts meet the criteria. If the Grand Canyon, for instance, can provide the larger context we desire, can a lakeside cottage or, for that matter, Disneyland? Goodin has an answer, and one that doesn't necessarily eliminate the cottage—although it probably does disqualify the Magic Kingdom. He says that we should avoid debates about whether some human lifestyles are more "natural" than others. Since humans are a part of nature, all human creations are natural, too. Some, though, are in better balance with other parts of nature; they are integrated into the larger setting in such a way that we can derive satisfaction from reflection

---

[22]Gooden, Robert, *Green Political Theory* (Cambridge: Blackwell, 1992), p. 45.

upon that greater context. Ultimately, Goodin concludes that what we should demand of context-providing artifacts is not that they leave nature "untouched by human hands" but, rather, that their touch is a light, or as he puts it, that it is a *loving* touch. What a "loving touch" upon nature entails is certainly open to interpretation, but our interpretations may converge if we consider what a "loving touch" upon anything—or anyone—entails. Applying loving touch upon our children, for instance, means we put their needs before our own, that we focus on what's best for them, that we hold their well-being as paramount. Analogously, applying a loving touch upon nature would involve asking ourselves a simple question before deciding how we should act: "In this situation, what is best for nature?"

This principle, that we should seek to apply a loving touch in our relationship to nature—that we should put her needs before our own—offers hope for resolving those ongoing dilemmas generated by the apparent conflict between human needs and nature's needs. We need not frame our debates in terms of loggers versus tree-spikers, developers versus farmers, or snowmobilers versus cross-country skiers. If what we're trying to apply is a loving touch, then there's a way that touch *can* be loving even if it is applied with a certain degree of technology. One can certainly imagine ways in which activities that are often decried by environmentalists—logging, hunting, home building—could be conducted in harmony with the overall natural context. For that matter, there's nothing about typically eco-friendly activities—camping, hiking, mountain biking—that guarantees they will be done with a loving touch. And what's especially important is that what constitutes a loving touch seems fairly easy to identify. All we have to do is look.

Here's an example.

I live in Los Angeles and I walk to work. (I'm one of about 8 in the city of 8 million who does so, but then again, my job is only three blocks from my house.) On my way, I pass by two homes, side-by-side, whose yards are in similar states of flux. It is during one of

Southern California's periodic winter droughts and water is being rationed, so lots of people are struggling to keep their lawns green. Even though these houses are just little Hollywood bungalows, with squares of unpaved ground in front of them no bigger than two small parking spaces, their owners each spend a lot of time and effort trying to overcome the unprecedently dry conditions.

Almost every day, on my way to work, I see an elderly Asian woman tending to the yard on the left. She has a big green garbage can and seems to spend most of her time cutting out squares of dead, brown turf and tossing them into this canister. As the weeks go on, her yard becomes more and more bare, like the head of a man going bald, while the barrel appears to get fuller and fuller, like the belly of that same man growing fatter and fatter.

Usually, on my way home, I see a middle-aged white guy—rather bald and stout himself—in the yard on the right. Generally, he has a wheelbarrow in which there is fertilizer and a big spray bottle of weed-killer. He pushes the wheelbarrow around dumping fertilizer on the growing number of bald patches in his yard, spraying them with chemicals of one sort or another and swearing at the city for prohibiting him from watering.

By late April, when the drought has been going on for over six months and when in a normal year, both lawns would have been verdant carpets, the battle appears lost. The Asian woman's yard has a few straggly strands of weeds and brush left; she now has not one, but three bulging trashcans full of its remains. Her bald neighbor's yard is as smooth and brown as a baseball diamond infield; his wheelbarrow and spray canisters lay near his front steps, defeated.

One Friday evening around that time, a cement mixer appears in the bald man's driveway. I assume it means he is going to have his sidewalk repaired or his basement refinished. But when I pass by his house on Monday morning, I discover the real reason he has hired the truck: his entire yard has been paved over, from end to end, in great, lumpy chunks of hardened concrete. It looks like the truck has just dumped its load at the sidewalk and that the wet cement has been quickly shoveled over the dirt. The effect is very much like the surface of the moon, except that, in a nod to the yard's former glory, the entire concrete slab has been spraypainted green. The heat rising off it, even at 8:30 in the morning, is intense. The paint still smells a bit and standing there, I feel slightly woozy. It is almost as if I can feel the earth choking under all that weight; my own breath seems to come up short in my throat.

At that moment, the bald man steps outside, catching me staring at his "lawn." "Looks good, don't it?" he asks defiantly.

"Uh . . . well . . . I've never seen anything quite like it, that's for sure," I manage.

The man comes down from his porch and surveys the painted concrete. "Never have to worry about mowing, fertilizing, or weeding ever again." He stamps on his cement and raises his fists victoriously. "I win! Don't care if it never rains."

A couple of weeks later, though, it does. A May storm lasts nearly a week, soaking the parched terrain and sending cars hurtling into each other all over the L.A. freeways.

On the morning of the second day of rain, the Asian woman is out in front of her house. She has tumbled over one of her garbage cans and is shoveling a rich, dark compost out of it onto her muddy yard. By evening, all three cans are empty and so thick is the black ooze covering her lawn that it looks like a cake with chocolate icing. By the time the rainstorm ends, green shoots are emerging all over. And in a month or so, when the June heat has already begun fading her neighbor's green yard to a dullish gray, the Asian woman's lawn looks like the 18th fairway at an expensive country club golf course.

Comparing these two approaches to yard care, isn't it obvious whose touch was more loving? Wouldn't any of us recognize the Asian woman's way of dealing with the situation as one that seemed more attuned to the needs of the natural world? And wouldn't we agree that the loving touch employed by the Asian woman was better?

If we can apply this principle to something as particular as urban horticulture, why can't we apply it as a general rule in our lives? Doesn't it make sense to use the notion of a loving touch as a way to help us figure out how we ought to behave? If it's so easy to see, shouldn't we use it? As hard as it is to figure out the right thing to do, isn't it reasonable to appeal to nature in this way as our oracle?

Philosophers Get the Last Word

Many philosophers would caution us about drawing any sort of conclusions from nature about the way we ought to behave. Eighteenth-century philosopher David Hume is famous for observing that it is a mistake to infer an "ought" from an "is." Facts about the world don't imply moral responsibilities. Even if we could, for instance, identify exactly what a loving touch upon nature was, it wouldn't automatically follow that we'd feel we ought to apply it. For Hume, this is essentially because the rational part of our beings—our minds—never gives us *any* motivation. It is only the emotional part—our hearts—that impels us to behave in one way or another. Nothing we *know*, then, can stimulate us to act; it's only what we *feel* that does so.

Moralists, though, observes Hume, are always trying to derive conclusions about what we ought to do from the way things are. He says this is illegitimate because "ought" isn't a matter of facts; it's a matter of feelings. To illustrate, he famously claims that it's not contrary to reason to prefer the destruction of the world to the scratching of one's little finger. Pretty radical claim: even if it were an established fact that the choice to scratch our little finger would result in the destruction of the world, it wouldn't necessarily follow that we'd perceive a moral responsibility to refrain from scratching it.

Twentieth-century philosophers make a similar point when they talk about something called "the naturalistic fallacy." This is the fallacy of assuming that there is a unique natural property that makes something right or wrong, good or bad, or whatever. It's considered fallacious because we can always wonder whether something with that property really *is* right or wrong, good or bad, or whatever. Suppose, for instance, we decided that it was a loving touch upon nature that makes right acts right. We could still recognize something as a loving touch and yet reasonably ask ourselves whether we ought to do it.

What this all boils down to is the claim that there's a difference between facts about the natural world and facts[23] about morality. The former just sort of "sit there"; the latter, though, have a motivational force: they tell us what we ought or ought not to do. In philosophical terms, the former are descriptive properties, the latter, normative properties. Descriptive properties merely describe; normative properties have an action-guiding force—they tell us how we should or shouldn't behave. And since descriptive properties can never capture the normative dimension of moral terms like "right" and "wrong," it's impossible for any descriptive property ever to imply some way we should be. Thus, even if it's an undeniable fact that my elderly Asian neighbor applied a loving touch upon nature while my bald neighbor didn't, it still doesn't follow that we ought to be more like her.

There are at least two ways to respond to this, though. First is to notice that some descriptive terms do seem to guide our actions in one way or another. Words like "kind" or "compassionate," or "thoughtful" describe behavior but also endorse it. Descriptions like "mean" or "callous" or "intolerant" carry with them an implicit rejection of such behavior. Philosophers call these "thick" moral concepts because they are both descriptive and normative. In this way, some facts about the world do tell us how we ought or ought not to be. When we identify someone as an "arrogant, self-centered fool" we may, after all, simply be stating the facts. But it would take someone equally arrogant, self-centered, and foolish to ask if we thought that person represented an admirable model of human behavior.

---

[23] Lots of people will argue whether moral "facts" exist at all, but that's another discussion.

Second, if we understand moral facts on the analogy with color we've been exploring—as properties that depend on a relationship between the viewing subject and the viewed object—then it's perfectly straightforward for such facts to imply certain "oughts." For us to perceive something as the right thing to do already includes the recognition of our responsibility to do it. If we don't recognize it, then we don't perceive it as right. To refer back to the example from above, a genuine understanding that a given gesture represented a loving touch upon nature would quite simply *entail* our obligation to perform it. The very meaning of "loving touch" would include that necessary subjective response on the part of the observer. Someone who said to me, "I recognize that your Asian neighbor touched nature lovingly and your bald neighbor didn't, but I don't know which of them did a better thing" would be talking nonsense. It would be like saying, "I see that your Asian neighbor is holding a four-sided polygon and your bald neighbor has a three-sided one, but I don't know which of them has a triangle."

An illuminating comparison can be made with humor. What does it mean to say that something is funny? If we say it sincerely, we mean something about *both* the thing being referred to and ourselves: we mean that it makes us laugh. When I say that Charlie Chaplin's *Modern Times* is a funny movie, I'm referring to that relationship between the movie and me. I'm stating a fact of the matter, but it's a fact that encompasses not only the Little Tramp's celluloid adventure but also my response to it. It would be strange for me to say, "I honestly think *Modern Times* is a very funny movie; there's nothing in it that makes me smile." The motivation to laughter is built into my assessment of the movie's funniness.

The same thing goes for my sincere statement that something is the right thing to do. If I say, for instance, that "parental love is good," I'm not merely identifying a feature of parental love, I'm also revealing something about my reaction to it: I'm saying that I think parents ought to love their children. For me to claim this *without* having that reaction would be to misuse the term "good." It would be like calling something a "triangle" without referring to a three-sided polygon.

Thus, if we understand morality on the model we've been exploring, it's mistaken to insist that facts don't imply obligations. If those facts include fact about us, then it's perfectly reasonable to say that they carry with them an obligation on our part to behave one way or another.

But of course, all this is far easier said than done. In the real world, all kinds of conflicts and confusions make it difficult to identify alleged moral facts and the supposed obligations that follow from them.

What we want to do often gets in the way of what we know we ought to do. Our desires tug us in a different direction than our knowledge of what's right. Our head tells us one thing; our heart— or some other, less respectable organ—tells us something else -entirely.

So what do we do in such situations? How do we overcome our feelings so we can manage to do the right thing? Or do we?

In the next chapter, we'll examine these questions. So turn the page if you feel like it—or if you just know that you should.

Chapter Six

Right on Purpose

Doing Right by Yourself

How to Be Half-Wicked

The Greeks had a word for it: *akrasia*. Sometimes translated as "weakness of will." Sometimes as "incontinence." Sometimes not translated at all.

However you put it, though, it's a phenomenon we're all familiar with. Think of those situations in which you know the right thing to do but in which your desire for something else overcomes you. You're fully aware of what you should do, but you can't help yourself. You know that what you're about to do is bad, but you do it anyway.

Aristotle talks at length of *akrasia*, contrasting his view of human nature with Socrates'. For Socrates, *akrasia* is impossible; the only reason people do bad things is because they are ignorant. If we know what's right, we'll do it. The idea that we could have knowledge of what's morally required of us but still not fulfill that requirement makes no sense to Socrates.

But as Aristotle points out, this plainly contradicts the apparent facts of human behavior.[24] Socrates is either naive or overly optimistic about the way people are. Consider the usually staid and respectable businessperson who can't resist the occasional temptation to overcharge on an expense account. Or the normally faithful spouse who turns a deaf ear to good judgment and has a passionate fling with an office co-worker. Or the parent who recognizes that the right thing to do is to read baby another story but who can't manage to get up off the comfortable couch and do so.

As for me, I always think of an event that occurred more than 30 years ago now. I was only a child, but I did know something about what was right and what wasn't. Even so, I couldn't stop myself from being bad—it just felt *so good.*

We're vacationing from our vacation in Europe. We've been living in Holland for six months while my dad takes a sabbatical from work. Right now, though, we're traveling through Germany, returning from two weeks in Scandinavia. We've been in the car for what seems like months, driving down one interminable two-lane road after another, with never a Dairy Queen or McDonald's to stop at. I'm sick of sitting in the back seat with my sister, sick of hearing my parents "ooh" and "aah" over a bunch of boring old buildings, and sick of being away from home, television, and baseball.

At 11 years old, I'm aware of the difference between right and wrong. I know that some things get you in trouble: playing with matches, messing with the stuff on Dad's desk, hitting your sister. I know that other things get you in good graces: cleaning up your room, telling the truth, helping your mom with the dishes. Perhaps I haven't completely internalized the difference; maybe I'm just motivated by avoiding punishment and earning praise. But be that as

---

[24]Aristotle, *Nichomachean Ethics,* Book VII, part ii.

it may, I certainly know that there are some things I'm supposed to do and some I'd better not.

One of those in the "not" group is disappearing from my parents' sight the moment we check into a motel. So at the moment, I'm hanging out in our room as they get settled in and unpack. Not that there's anywhere to go, anyway. We're staying at a roadside rest stop just off some highway in the middle of Germany. The motel grounds butt right up against the tarmac. There's only a ditch and a cyclone fence separating us from cars speeding by. If this were America, the place would at least have a pool or a dog run. Here, the only amenity, as far as I can see, is a small square of concrete near the reception area. I guess you're supposed to put out your lawn chairs so you can have a good view of the Mercedes streaming past.

The room doesn't even have a TV set. All I can get on the radio is a bunch of men barking at each other in German. I keep twisting the dial but manage only static. Turning it up louder doesn't do anything but earn the attention of my mother.

"If you're going to make a nuisance of yourself, could you do it quietly, at least?"

"This place stinks," I complain. "They don't even have a pool."

"I don't think that would make much difference," my father points out, quite reasonably. "It's barely sixty degrees. You'd freeze your touchas off."

"Well, at least I wouldn't have to sit around this stupid room."

"So, go outside," says my mom. "I'm sure you can get into some kind of mischief if you try hard enough."

As a matter of fact, I don't even have to try very hard. But I don't think the mischief I find is exactly what my mother had in mind.

My sister—who took Mom's cue to escape the room along with me—and I have wandered in a circle all the way around to the back of the motel. We've found nothing at all of any interest. Until now.

Sitting on a dusty patch of earth by the motel's back door is a broken-down motorcycle. It has its front wheel removed and is supported by a concrete block under the front fork. All around it are parts of various sorts: a spark plug here, a cylinder head there, half of a gas tank over there. Littered among these is a selection of tools, including a screwdriver, a wrench, and several sizes of pliers.

"Cool!" I exclaim and climb immediately onto the motorcycle's seat. I take the handlebars and work the throttle like I'm riding it.

"I don't think you should do that," says my sister.

I have a feeling that she's right, but I don't let on. "Why not?" I ask defiantly. "It's broken, anyways."

"It looks like it's being fixed," says my sister, motioning to the tools and parts spread around.

"No way. This bike is toast." I'm lying and I know it. I can tell perfectly well that someone is working on the motorcycle. But something has gotten into me. I suddenly feel this compelling desire to do what I know I shouldn't.

I reach over and pick up a large crescent wrench from the ground. "Here, I'll show you." With a quick flick of my wrist, I smash the motorcycle's headlamp. "See? It's totally trashed."

"I don't think so," says my sister, backing away. "And even if it isn't, you still shouldn't wreck it."

I know she's right. I know what I'm doing is wrong, but there's something indescribably satisfying about my small power to destroy. I shiver at the feeling of the heavy wrench crunching through the brittle headlamp, the tinkle of the falling shards as they fall down upon each other. I give the lamp another smash. This time my wrist catches on a broken piece, cutting me slightly. The trickle of blood that begins slithering down my forearm only adds to my excitement.

"David, you'd better stop."

She doesn't have to tell me. I know I should. Part of me even wants to. But the strange pleasure I'm getting out of being bad has taken over. I bring the wrench above the glass-encased odometer that sits between the motorcycle's handlebars. I swing it down with all my might. The glass shatters and the loops of numbers that turn to show the passage of miles splinter apart. One of them gets caught around the head of the wrench. I twist the tool trying to get it free. The number loop curls into a figure-eight. I tug at it, lifting the entire broken odometer out of its casing. It remains stuck to the wrench like a hooked fish. I swing it around, laughing at its tenacious grip. Even as I smash it again and again on the edge of the hole where it used to reside it won't let go.

I bring the wrench over my head to slam it down one more time. But as I do, over the noise of my breathing, I hear a different sound rising. I look to my right to see a small, dark-haired woman bursting from the motel's back door. She is screaming at me in German. I can't understand a word she is saying—but I don't have to. I know what she's saying: that what I've been doing is terribly wrong. I don't need a translator to confirm this.

I throw down the wrench and run away as fast as I can. I scurry across the motel's side lawn, darting and weaving like commandos in army shows on TV. When I get to the ditch by the road, I slide into it, hunkering down so only the very top of my head shows over the edge.

Hidden by the weeds and brambles, I can see everything that's going on. The German woman marches over to my parents' room and bangs on the door. My dad comes out and listens, nodding his head as she gesticulates wildly. She practically drags him away behind the motel, probably, I figure, to go look at the motorcycle. My mother comes out of the room and talks to my sister. I can tell she is dismayed by what she is hearing. She lights a cigarette and smokes it, surveying the landscape with her hand cupped over her eyes. My sister skips around her, carefree, doing every sibling's favorite "you're in trouble and I'm not" dance.

Eventually, my dad returns and talks to my mom. There's a lot of headshaking and sighing. My dad points toward the back of the motel and shrugs. He lights a cigarette, too, smoking it as he wanders around the motel grounds calling my name.

Dusk begins to settle and I get chilly in my hiding place. I inch up out of the ditch. My father, who has gone back and forth across the road a couple of times looking for me, catches my movement out of the corner of his eye.

He shouts my name and comes running straight at me.

I experience a strange rush of emotions. First and foremost, I'm scared. I know I've done a bad thing and that I'm in trouble. I'm fearful of what my father will do when he catches me. At the same time, though, I desperately want him to grab me and hold me. I want to be bundled up in his arms and protected—not only from the German woman, but also from myself.

I crumple to the ground, unable to either run toward or away from my father. He charges up and takes me in his arms.

"David," he says, breathing hard as he carries me back to the motel. "What were you thinking?"

I don't know if he means when I smashed the motorcycle or when I hid out. All I can do by way of response is to cry.

"We'll talk about this tomorrow," says my dad. "Right now, you need to go to bed."

I get a quick bath and then turn in. In my travel journal, which I dutifully fill out every night before sleeping, I write: 'Today was the stupidest day of my life. I can't even write about how dumb I was. How could I ever do that? Why didn't I stop? Will I ever be able to forget this? Will I ever be able to live this down? Will I ever be able to be happy again?"

Obviously, I have been able to live it down, and I'm pleased to say that it wasn't very long before I was able to be happy again. But I've never forgotten the incident and especially that very strange feeling of simultaneously knowing the right thing to do but being unable to do it. I've experienced it many times subsequently—for instance, knowing I ought not take that last piece of pie in the fridge but reaching for it anyway or realizing I should pay my friend back the five bucks I owe him but spending it on video games instead—and each time I do, I experience some measure of that odd mixture of surprise and excitement: I can't believe I'm actually doing this, but I can't stop myself from doing it.

Does this make me a wicked person? Not exactly. Aristotle would say that I'm only half-wicked. *Akrasia* is not a vice for Aristotle; it's a kind of weakness.

By contrast, someone who is self-indulgent, someone who pursues pleasures to excess without any concern for right and wrong, is bad. For one thing, self-indulgent people have no regrets for what they've done. Weak-willed people, on the other hand, suffer remorse when we succumb to our desires and fail to do what we know we ought to. We lose sleep over our inability to make the right choice even when we can see what it is. For this reason, Aristotle says we are "curable." Unlike self-indulgent people, we can learn to overcome the desires that lead us astray. We can draw upon the regret that we feel to steer us in the right direction.

The question, of course, is "how?" And the answer, not surprisingly, is "it's much easier said than done."

The Pleasures of Virtue

For Aristotle, virtuous people take pleasure in being virtuous. The real test of someone's character, therefore, is what they enjoy doing most. Bad people take delight in doing bad things; good people find the greatest joy in doing what's right.

Someone who is a brute will get his kicks from behaving brutishly. Someone who is self-indulgent about his appetite will be happiest when he's stuffing his face. A virtuous person, on the other hand, will want to be pleasant to others, will want to be moderate in her consumption—not because she *has* to, but because that's what she finds most pleasurable.

Weak-willed people are better than brutes and pigs because they at least recognize what virtue requires, even if they're unable to restrain their desires for lesser goods.

Strong-willed, or what some translators call "continent" people are a step up. They too, have the desire for the baser pleasures but are self-controlled enough not to indulge. We might picture here a person on a diet. He would dearly love that second piece of cheesecake, but—drawing upon all his willpower—declines. The desire for overindulgence is still there, but with teeth clenched and fists doubled up, he holds it in check.

According to Aristotle, though, the truly virtuous person

experiences no such tension. She quite simply does not want the second piece of cake. One is enough for her; she would take no pleasure in overindulging. Her appetites have been trained so that what makes her most happy is what is indeed most virtuous. Unlike the vast majority of us who are constantly having to force ourselves against our desires to do the right thing, virtuous people actually desire to do what's right. They are courageous, generous, friendly, temperate, and so on not because (or at least, not *only* because) they realize they should be. They embody all these admirable character traits because happiness for them entails being good people.

No doubt one could argue that Aristotle has a Pollyanna-ish conception of human nature. Where does he get off claiming that anyone *really* gets more pleasure out of being good than being bad? That's just naive. Look around at the world. Who's happier: the guy volunteering at the soup kitchen or Dennis Rodman? Who would most people in the world rather be?

Granted, Aristotle's claim is something of a tough sell. But if we introspect honestly, we might find that, as a matter of fact, it does correspond to our own experience. The times we've felt the highest pleasures are indeed those times when we've done the best things. Or at least—if my experience is any gauge—we never feel as good as we thought we would when our pleasure is based on doing something bad.

In Mrs. McConnan's second-grade class, I am definitely the teacher's pet. But there's a reason for that: I'm funny, I'm smart, and I absolutely adore Mrs. McConnan. I'll do anything from washing the blackboards after school to feeding the classroom chameleon just to earn her favor. Most of all, though, I'm an utter glory-hound. I desperately crave the attention and praise of my classmates and teacher. I'm always going above and beyond what our assignments call for just to get that extra pat on the back, that special notice that sets me apart from everyone else. It's not that I have to be better, it's just that I have to be recognized. And if that means I have to slop soapy water on a chalky blackboard when my friends are out playing, then so be it.

It also means that I'm not adverse to doing things I know I shouldn't if will win me that extra attention. Like the time I brought my dad's stethoscope in to class for show and tell, even though he'd told me never to touch it when he wasn't around. Or when I snuck back in the classroom at recess to snoop at the list of words on Mrs. McConnan's desk so I could be sure of winning the afternoon spelling bee.

Or this time, when I'm not only plagiarizing, but lying about it in order to be the first one in class to finish our current poetry and drawing assignment.

Mrs. McConnan has asked us to write a poem and illustrate it—no easy task for 7-year-olds for whom reading itself is a challenge. Finished assignments will be posted around the room for parents to see on tonight's Open House Night. And yet, while my classmates are all still chewing on their pencils trying to come up with a few simple rhymes, I'm already coloring in my picture. My poem is long done. It has literally written itself, flowing out of my pencil like water from a spigot. It took no time at all to compose; as fast as I could write it, there it was on paper. But that's not surprising, really. It's not as if I had to make it up. I'm simply repeating a poem that I misread and memorized the other day when I was at the library. It goes like this: "Those who write on laboratory walls/Roll their shirts into little balls."

My picture features a scientist in a lab coat, standing in his laboratory whose walls are covered with writing. He is, as the poem describes, rolling his shirt up into a little ball.

I'm quite pleased with the drawing, especially the way I've depicted the laboratory, with all sorts of beakers and burners and electrical cables. I sketch in a few lightning bolts for a finishing touch and take my masterpiece over to Mrs. McConnan's desk to show it off. She's quite impressed that I'm already finished.

"Can we hang it up on the wall now?" I ask, passing her my work.

"My goodness, David, that certainly was quick," she says, taking the paper. "You must be a natural poet to have written yours so fast."

I feel the surge of pride that comes from being recognized as something special. It's tempered by my knowledge that the praise is undeserved, but Mrs. McConnan's attention is almost enough to make me forget that I didn't really write the poem. If she keeps it up, I'll soon be able to convince myself that the work is all mine.

But when she takes a look at my paper, her face falls. She wrinkles her brow and looks at me.

"David, did you write this yourself?" she asks.

"Yes," I lie, wondering how in the world she could be suspicious.

"You didn't have any help?"

My mind is racing. There is only one way Mrs. McConnan could know that I'm lying. And that's if she was in the same stall as me in the boy's room at the library. But that's impossible! My secret has to be safe.

"No. I wrote it all myself."

Mrs. McConnan, bless her heart, doesn't press the issue. Instead, she tries a diversion. "You know, we need to check on the spelling of 'laboratory.' Why don't you try writing another poem in the meantime?"

I've got a better solution. I trot over to the big dictionary that sits on a pedestal by the window. I look up 'laboratory' and write down the correct spelling.

Mrs. McConnan is a bit surprised to see me back so soon. And she's even more astonished to see that I haven't brought her a new poem, but rather, a small slip of paper with the word 'laboratory' on it.

"See? I spelled it right," I say, handing her the paper. "Can we hang my poem up now?"

Mrs. McConnan looks at the crumpled slip and then back at me. "I don't think so just yet. It might make the other students who aren't finished yet feel bad."

I don't understand her reluctance to post my work. And I don't understand why I feel so hollow even though I finished first.

"I still think you ought to try writing another poem," suggests Mrs. McConnan gently.

I return to my seat, still half-expecting the rush of pride I was expecting from seeing my poem posted ahead of all the others. It doesn't come. I fidget in my chair, looking around at my classmates hard at work. Finally, with nothing else to do, I take out a piece of paper and begin doodling a few words on it.

The next thing I know, Mrs. McConnan is tapping me on the shoulder.

"David, it's time to go home."

"Wait. I'm almost done," I say.

One last line and I finish the poem I've been working on all afternoon. It's about my family pet, and begins, "I have a cat/Who doesn't wear a hat."

"What about your picture?" asks Mrs. McConnan. "Everyone else is already done with theirs." She motions about the room, where 30 of my classmates' illustrated poems are now hanging.

"Can I do it tonight and bring it tomorrow?"

Mrs. McConnan isn't worried about it being late; she's only concerned about my happiness. "You don't mind that yours won't be up for Open House Night?"

Strangely, I don't. The pleasure associated with this poem is completely different than the first one I "wrote." It has nothing to do with having other people appreciate it. In fact, I don't even care. All I know is that I feel really good for having worked so hard on it and created something that's entirely my own. This kind of pride completely fills my chest whereas the other just stuck in my throat. Somehow it's much better. More real. Like the difference between eating one of my grandma's homemade ginger cookies and a Sunshine Hydrox wannabe-Oreo.

Even though I didn't have the vocabulary to describe the difference in pleasures I experienced between turning in the plagiarized poem and writing my own, I could easily distinguish between the two. The feeling I got from doing the right thing was more authentic, more real, and more lasting. It wasn't based on anyone else's reaction; it wasn't ephemeral. It felt good no matter what anyone else said or did. By contrast, the other pleasure was purely contingent. If Mrs. McConnan didn't react positively, then I wouldn't feel anything. I depended on her praise to make me feel good. The pleasure associated with virtue couldn't be taken away from me; the other was never even mine in the first place.

The idea that there are different qualities of pleasure may be a peculiarly philosophical notion. Psychologists may rightly argue that, as matter of scientific fact, pleasure is pleasure. It's nothing more than a physiological state; whatever feels good does, in fact, feel good. Granted, there are different *degrees* of pleasure, but it's a mistake to think there are different *kinds*.

Philosophers, however, have long argued that some pleasures are better than others. From the ancient Greeks on, it has been something of a philosophical truism that the pleasure that comes from philosophizing, for instance, is better than the one you get from, say, making lots of money.

The 19th-century utilitarian philosopher John Stuart Mill is quite explicit in his claim that pleasures come in different qualities. Sensual pleasures are not as good as intellectual pleasures; the pleasures of the body are not as good as those of the mind. This is the basis of his famous quote: "It is better to be a human being dissatisfied than a pig satisfied; better to be Socrates dissatisfied than a fool satisfied."[25]

When asked what proof he has for this claim, his answer is similar to what my example above intended to illustrate. You just have to ask people who have experienced both kinds. Mill says that it is an unquestionable fact that those who are acquainted with both kinds of pleasures will always prefer the higher ones. None of us would consent to be changed into an animal even if we were promised the full measure of that animal's pleasures. Similarly, no

---

[25]Mill, John Stuart, "Utilitarianism" (1861).

intelligent human—someone who knows what the higher pleasures feel like—would trade places with an ignoramus, even the
happiest ignoramus in the world.

Not everyone agrees with Mill. I've heard a number of people
say they would gladly be happy fools. "I'd love to be completely
satisfied just lying in the sun like my dog," they argue. "Ignorance
is bliss."

Perhaps it is, but in response, I can only contrast it with my
own experience (and that of thousands of years of philosophers),
which leads me, like Mill, to aspire instead to Socrates' dissatisfac-
tion. Sure it would be great to be a happy pig—if only I were a pig.
But since—fortunately or not—I'm not, my preferred option is to
make every effort to experience the better pleasures, even if in
doing so I often end up dissatisfied.

All of this, then, is to argue in a rather roundabout way that
Aristotle is right: the pleasures that result from doing the right
thing *are* better than those that come from being bad. And *if*
Aristotle is right, then we have some hope of learning to appreciate
those better pleasures, of preferring them to the lesser ones, and,
consequently, of coming to more consistently be motivated to *do,*
not just to *know,* the right thing to do.

Infamously, however, Aristotle doesn't give much practical ad-
vice for how to go about learning to appreciate virtuous behavior.
Basically, one becomes a virtuous person by behaving virtuously.
It's a matter of training, like learning to play a musical instrument.
The way you get better is through practice. And presumably, the
more you practice, the better you get.

Tips for Preferring the Preferable

But how in the world do we practice being virtuous? Doing the
right thing isn't like shooting a basket or hitting a tennis ball. We
can't go out on the court after work and knock around a few virtues
with our friends.

Or can we?

If improving our ability to do the right thing involves practicing, then we can at least do as Aristotle advises: we can emulate virtuous people. We can do as they do, follow their lead, imitate their behavior.

We may not feel the same motivation they do, we may not even understand why they're doing what they're doing, but we can nevertheless behave as they behave. And in doing so, if Aristotle is right, we will slowly but surely train ourselves to be like them. We will become virtuous by practicing to be like a virtuous person.

This is more or less the theory behind instruction in many martial arts or body movement disciplines. In a yoga or tai chi class, students try to mimic the poses of their teacher. At first, they merely approximate what the master does. But eventually, after repeated attempts, students begin to make the postures their own. Instead of working from the "outside-in," copying what they are seeing, they begin to work from the "inside-out," feeling the movements originate in their own bodies.

My next door neighbor Louis, an 84-year-old gentleman from Louisiana, is teaching me to garden this way. Louis *is* a gardener. He doesn't say much, but it's pretty obvious from his character that he knows all there is to know about backyard farming. He's out there every morning doing what needs to be done to make his corn, beans, collard greens, tomatoes, and other vegetables grow. I just watch and do whatever he does. When he adds peat moss to his soil, I add some to mine. When he pulls weeds and sifts out rocks, so do I. The days that he is in his garden watering at 6:30 A.M., I'm in mine with a hose at 10:00. Most of the time, I don't know why I'm doing what I'm doing; I just do it because Louis does, trusting that he has a reason. Occasionally, though, I understand the purpose behind the activity I'm emulating. And sometimes I even manage to predict what Louis will do and can undertake those same activities without his help. In those rare moments, I get a taste of what it really is to be a gardener. My hope is that as the years go by and I continue to follow his lead, I will eventually experience more of such moments. I will finally internalize Louis' lessons and make them my own. And someday, perhaps when I'm 84 myself, I honestly will be able to say that like Louis, I am truly a gardener, too.

Now, one could argue that it's a lot easier to become a good gardener than a good person. By emulating Louis, I can improve my ability to grow vegetables, but can I say the same thing about my ability to do the right thing?

One obvious difficulty is that it's easy to see who the good gardeners are; it's not so simple to determine who the good people are. I can assure you that I don't choose a bad role model for my gardening aspirations by looking at that person's tomatoes and peas. Unfortunately, I can't be so certain about my choice of moral exemplar. Bad things happen to good people and vice versa; it would be a mistake, therefore, to simply model my behavior on that of individuals who have achieved our culturally-accepted conception of success. Lots of rich and successful people would provide poor examples to emulate; many individuals who are struggling to make ends meet would be excellent role models. How then, am I to make a wise choice about whose lead I should follow—especially since I'm very apt to make a poor choice about the person whose character I think is best? And what am I to do in the meantime while I'm searching for the one who will show me how I ought to be?

One thing that's clear is that it won't do to simply wait around hoping to be shown the way. We need to make a regular effort to develop our appetite for the authentically good. Every practice requires preparation. Musicians review their scales every day before playing real tunes. Visual artists clean their brushes and sweep their studios as a kind of mental and physical warm-up. Similarly, those of us who consider virtue one of our arts can also engage in activities that prepare us for our "real" work.

Here then, are a few "scales" to work on as part of an ongoing process of training ourselves to be the best persons we know how to be.

Nobody's perfect. So it's important, if we hope to improve our ability to perceive and choose the right thing to do, that we admit to others—and ourselves—that we're not. Face it: even the best people screw up sometimes. Fear or laziness or just bad timing make us do the wrong thing. This is perfectly natural. There's nothing wrong with making mistakes; the only shame is in not learning from them.

When my daughter Amelia was just a few months old, I stupidly put her on the dining room table in her carseat. I turned my back for few seconds to grab my coat and she hurled herself out of the seat and onto the floor, knocking the wind out of her and bruising her chest. As I lifted her off the ground and rocked her tears away, my wife, Jennifer, who had been downstairs in her basement studio working hard against an important deadline, appeared and asked what happened.

I was scared for my daughter, embarrassed by how stupid I'd been to leave her unattended, and worried that Jennifer would be sufficiently concerned to stop working and miss her deadline. So, I lied.

"Oh. Nothing. She was sitting in her carseat and tumbled over."

Jennifer sized the baby and me up. "Was she on the table?" she asked with horror in her voice.

"Oh, no," I lied. "What do you think, I'm stupid? Of course not. Don't be silly." I rocked her head higher so Jennifer could see. "See? She's fine. Really. Don't worry."

Jennifer looked at me skeptically but then backed out of the room. I breathed a sigh of relief and uttered a silent wish that my baby really was all right.

A couple days later, when Amelia was all better, I admitted to Jennifer what had actually happened. She was justifiably furious.

"How dare you keep that information from me! What if she had really been hurt? Suppose she started coughing up blood or something when you weren't here? How would I have known what to tell the doctor?"

I had no answer, no defense. I knew there was no excuse for what I had done. It was stupid enough to have left Amelia in her carseat like that, but it was just flat wrong to have lied to Jennifer about it. Any of the seven moral prisms would have helped me see that. Lying about what happened disrespected Jennifer's dignity; it had undesirable consequences; no one I admire would have done it; it restricted Jennifer's freedom; it negatively affected the caring relationship between us; it wasn't in my self-interest ultimately, and if everyone I know knew I was lying, I wouldn't have.

There was nothing I could say other than, "I'm sorry. I was wrong. I'll never do that again." And this time, at least, I wasn't lying.

- *Feel Guilt and Shame*
One of the many ways we can divide up the world is between cultures whose morals are shame-based and ones whose morality is guilt-based. In shame-based cultures, like that of Ancient Greece, atonement for wrongdoing has a public dimension. Wrongdoers are ostracized by those to whom they have done wrong; when you're bad, you have to appear before the community—figuratively, at least—and have shame heaped upon you by others. In guilt-based cultures, like that of the contemporary West, atonement is much more private. When you do something wrong, you turn inward, escape from public view, and wrack your own self with guilt.

The philosopher Allan Gibbard theorizes that the emotions of guilt and shame have an evolutionary basis. Both arose as a way for people to deal with bad treatment they expected to receive from others. Guilt developed in response to situations in which punishment was expected. Shame came about in response to situations in which neglect was portended. Anger and neglect have different remedies, says Gibbard. When others are angry at us, we need to placate them through apology, restitution, and contrition. When people disdain us, we need to either withdraw or display our powers, to show that we can contribute to ongoing cooperative ventures. Guilt, concludes Gibbard, tends toward amends; shame toward the development of one's powers.[26]

Woody Allen, in the movie *Manhattan*, sings the praises of guilt to his friend, Yale, who has recently restarted his romance with the woman whom Woody has been dating. "Guilt is good," he says. "It keeps us from doing horrible things."

The same can be said for shame, which—at the very least—keeps us from doing horrible things more than once. Feeling ashamed of having done something wrong, recognizing that others have a right to be angry at us for doing what we did, enables us to rectify our behavior the next time around. Feeling guilty over our moral failings provides us with room for introspective reflection so we can better understand how and why we screwed up . . . and presumably, do better next time.

- *Do as You Say, Not as You Do*
We all fall into patterns of behavior that we repeat without really thinking about them. We develop a habit of doing something and, even if we know it's wrong, keep doing it out of habit. We may want to stop, but by then, the behavior has become so much a part of our personality that we can't. It feels hypocritical to even talk about changing. So, we just keep doing what we've always been doing in spite of the fact we know we shouldn't.

In high school, I had a summer job working in a laboratory where doctors were doing experiments on the effects of amphetamines on monkeys and rats. Part of my job involved injecting the animals with the various substances they were

---

[26]Gibbard, Allan, *Wise Choices, Apt Feelings* (Cambridge: Harvard University Press, 1990), p. 139.

being tested for. One day, for no particular reason, I put a few grains of methamphetamine into a gum wrapper and took it home with me. I gave it to a friend of mine who was into speed, and he said it was incredible. He paid me ten bucks to get him some more. Pretty soon, I was filching drugs from work almost daily. I don't exactly know why. I didn't need the money. I didn't need the anxiety and guilt. I didn't even want to keep doing it, but it had become something I just did. I told my friend I thought what we were doing was wrong. He said I had no right to make judgments. I was the one who was stealing; where did I get off saying anything about right and wrong? I didn't know how to respond. It seemed he had a point. What right did I have to say what ought to be when I was so imperfect myself? So I just kept nipping at the methamphetamine bottle, in spite of knowing that I ought not to. (Fortunately, the situation resolved itself when one of the graduate students at the laboratory was caught stealing rather large amounts of pharmaceuticals and much tighter controls were instituted.)

I believe many of us occasionally find ourselves in a similar situation. We want to do the right thing but can't because it feels forced or unnatural or completely out of character. In this case, though, the only thing to do may be to go ahead and do what we say should be done. So what if we haven't, as a general rule, lived up to the standards we preach? So what if we never have? A person has to start somewhere and it may as well be the same place we want to end up.

• Try It, You'll Like It

If acquiring virtue is a matter of training and practice, then we have to experience it in order to become virtuous. So it behooves us to try doing the right thing to see how it feels. It may be far more congenial than we previously imagined.

I remember the first time I went to a cocktail party with my wife after we were married. As a newlywed, I had decided that it would be inappropriate to flirt shamelessly with everyone at the party in what was my usual attempt at the time to either get lucky or get slapped. I was a little curious as to how long I'd last at the party; it struck me as potentially a rather dreary way to spend an evening. But as it turned out, I had a great time. Instead of having to rush around trying to charm everyone, I was able to engage in a number of relatively deep and interesting conversations. Since my interactions with others weren't so goal-related, I was able to let them unfold naturally. I actually got to know some of the guests and felt they learned something about me, too. More important, I think, I learned something about myself as well.

- *Practice Daily… Almost*

Making a habit out of anything worthwhile requires regular, focused practice. To be a great musician, you need to pick up your instrument every day and play it, even on those days when you feel uninspired and lazy. To excel as an artist, you have to draw, paint, or sculpt at every opportunity, always honing your skills. In business, the people who succeed are generally those who work not only hard but consistently, making regular, steady progress toward their goals. The same goes for acquiring the habit of doing the right thing. We have to work on ourselves all the time, continually steering our desires into alignment with what we know we should do. It's a seven day a week, 24-hour a day job . . . almost.

We need to cut ourselves some amount of slack. Even the Creator took Sunday off. So it's equally important to allow ourselves some room for imperfection. We ought occasionally to take a rest. This doesn't mean that one day a week we go out and rob banks. It's only meant to remind us that it's okay to slip up from time to time. Doing something bad doesn't necessarily make you a bad person, especially if it's a mistake to be learned from. The main thing to keep in mind is that now and again, we all *will* do things we later realize we shouldn't have. How we handle those occasions and use them as an opportunity for growth is the real test of our character.

- *Do It for Nothing*
We've seen how self-interest and morality often conflict; sometimes, though, they work together. And, in fact, we regularly find ourselves in situations where the only reason we seriously consider doing the right thing is because we'll get something in return. We've all heard (or said) statements like: "I'm only keeping my promise to them so they'll keep their promises to me"; or "The reason I'm honoring the warranty is so my customer will buy from me again"; or "I'll do what I said I would do—but only if I get paid for it."

There's nothing wrong with this; it's not at all unreasonable to expect some benefit from doing what we ought to do. The problem though—and we've explored this before—is that if the *only* reason we're choosing the right thing is for the profit it brings us, then our likelihood of consistently choosing it is lessened.

So, if we want to improve our ability to not only perceive but to *choose* the right thing, then we should make it a point to do so in situations where it's not obviously in our advantage. Volunteering at community organizations, giving anonymously to charity, and donating blood are all examples of the kinds of behavior that can stimulate our "moral muscles" and make us more apt to do what's right for the right reasons and to take pleasure in the pleasures of virtue itself.

- *Paint with a Very Fine Brush*
In much of our lives, it's easier to say "no" than "yes." Saying "no" is safe; it usually doesn't require us to do anything. Saying "yes" calls upon us to act; it usually creates commitments we have to follow through on.

In the realm of ethics, "no" is the safe choice for the same reason. When we say "no" to something, we're less likely to do anything wrong. Identifying behaviors as things we ought not to do ensures that we'll avoid authentically bad choices. So, in the interest of safety, we may be apt to make "no" our default option; if something isn't explicitly right, we'll cover our backs by identifying it as wrong.

The danger of this, however, is twofold. First, it has the potential to cut us off from some of life's most intriguing possibilities. Many of the deeply meaningful experiences we will face between cradle and grave are somewhat ambivalent from a moral point of view. Eliminating them as possibilities without carefully exploring their specific features may exclude us from unique opportunities for growth and joy.

More important, by painting what's wrong with too broad a brush, we're apt to lose our appreciation for what really is morally objectionable. It's like the boy who cried "wolf." If we label too many things as "wolves," then we sacrifice our ability to distinguish between real wolves and what are only gray dogs. We want, in other words, to be as specific as possible about our "no's." Just because, for instance, it's wrong to steal money from a bank doesn't mean that it's equally objectionable to take a few paper clips home from work. We need to be able to maintain distinctions between what's permissible and what isn't. But if we overuse our power to censure, then it loses its power. If we say "no" too often, nobody listens—not even us.

- *Remember That the Better Doesn't Make the Good Bad*
Just because one choice or behavior is superior to others doesn't make the alternatives evil. Being a good person doesn't require that we *always* make the best choice; we can qualify as virtuous by consistently doing good things, even if they aren't necessarily unsurpassed in their excellence.

My friend Suzanne is the director of a community-based organization that teaches inner-city kids bicycle repair skills while giving them the opportunity to earn a free bike of their own. In her "spare" time, she volunteers at a Senior Citizens

Center and every summer participates in charity bike rides to raise money for research into cures for AIDS and muscular dystrophy. She's a vegan (consumes *no* animal products), doesn't own a car, and composts all her kitchen wastes. Plus, she's incredibly funny, sensitive, unassuming, and smart. Kids adore her, adults respect her, and animals are naturally drawn to her. In short, she makes us all look bad.

But that doesn't mean we *are* bad. Just because Suzanne is a paragon of virtue doesn't mean that the rest of us are slime. It's important to keep in mind that being good doesn't entail being perfect. We should be careful of holding ourselves to a standard we can't possibly achieve. Doing so is disheartening and makes us less likely to make *any* attempt to do the right thing.

Of course, we don't want to be too easy on ourselves; it won't do to set our sights so low that anything goes. However, we don't have to beat ourselves up just because we're not saints. It's enough to aspire—and to accomplish—to be merely good human beings.

• *Justify Yourself to 12 Year Olds*
One of the first things I do when I do philosophy with schoolkids is to develop a list of rules for philosophy. I have the students brainstorm about the principles they would like to be governed by. We get a big list on the blackboard and then the students choose five rules that will guide their community of inquiry. (Five seems to be about the right amount. Fewer won't set sufficient parameters for our discussions; more is too many to remember.) Because the students have come up with the rules themselves, they tend to be quite willing to follow them.

Usually, the rules are more reasonable than you might expect: "Don't talk when others are talking." "Keep your eyes on the speaker." "Respect yourself by respecting others." Occasionally, you get a strange one: "Don't spray your stinky breath in someone else's face."

In Ms. Hutchings' class, though, they really pushed it. One

of the rules the students came up with was, "Dave has to buy donuts every time he comes." Budding lawyers that they were, they closed off every loophole. The donuts had to be edible; they couldn't be mini donuts; I was to make sure there were enough to go around; and among the selection had to be a fair number of maple bars and glazed bear claws.

Initially, I balked at the rule. "This won't do," I said. "You'll have to come up with another one."

A chorus of "why's?" filled the room. "You said they were *our* rules!" shouted one student. "How come you get to change them if we're the ones supposed to be making them?"

I had to admit I didn't have an answer.

"That's not fair, then!" argued Brenna. "You have to give us a good reason. Otherwise you're not respecting us. And that's wrong."

Brenna was right, of course. I couldn't justify my position. I was merely trying to impose my preference on the group. So I agreed to bring donuts.

After having done so a couple of times, though, I was able to make a case for what was wrong with the rule. "I'm having to spend nearly $15 of my own money every time," I explained. "That hardly seems fair, does it?"

Students weren't too happy at the prospect of the donut pipeline running dry, but they saw my point. We renegotiated the rule so that I only had to *pick up* donuts—which the students would pay for—and only if we had made arrangements the previous week.

"You see," said Brenna when I expressed my gratitude for the modification, "we can figure out the right thing to do together. You just have to give us good reasons to work with."

Talk about being hoist by one's own petard. But I was glad to have been because it forced me to walk my talk. Twelve year olds may not be the most sophisticated philosophers in the world, but their bullshit detectors are world class. If you want to make sure you're demonstrating integrity in your choices about right and wrong, you will find no better test. Subject yourself to the scrutiny of sixth-graders. If you can explain to them your position and *why* you hold it, then there's a good chance it's pretty well justified.

- *Explore Other Traditions and Philosophies*
The ideas and suggestions in this book spring primarily from Western philosophy, and just a few small parts of it at that. Consequently, they promote an approach to deciding the right thing to do that is necessarily somewhat limited—and limiting.

But, of course, the perspectives offered herein are not the only ways to proceed. Rather, consider them starting points for further exploration.

The overriding message of the moral spectrum model is that by examining an issue through a number of different moral prisms, we are able to make better choices. It would be inconsistent with this model to suggest that the handful of approaches presented here represents anything like the last word on the subject.

The brief discussions of moral theory haven't been intended as a lesson in philosophical ethics; rather, they are merely meant to illustrate the rich variety of approaches we have—just in the West—for determining the right thing to do. And this is only by way of scratching the surface. Rights-based theories like those of John Locke or the contemporary philosopher Robert Nozick haven't been discussed. Nor have we given attention to theories of natural law such as those explored by the medieval philosopher Thomas Aquinas. And of course, the rich ethical traditions to be found in Christianity, Judaism, and other Western religions have only been referred to tangentially.

Moreover, there is much to be learned by exploring non-Western approaches to determining right and wrong. Philosophers and theologians working in Buddhist, Hindu, and Islamic traditions offer perspectives both similar to and unlike those of Western traditions. The ethical tradition in India known as Jainism, for instance, is founded in the belief that every entity in the world is sentient, whose distinguishing feature is consciousness along with vital energy and a happy disposition. As Pursottama Bilimoria points out, the Jaina ethical life thus becomes almost synonymous with the observance of a list of vows and austerities intended to prevent injury to these entities.[27] Jainas historically were so sensitive to even the accidental killing of living matter that they would strain their water to avoid drinking any creatures that might be in it and wear masks to keep from inhaling microscopic entities. This extreme asceticism ends up requiring such self-sacrifice that it represents a complete reversal of egoism. While very few of us would be willing to adopt such a program ourselves, it nevertheless expands our moral palette to consider such a unique perspective on things.

And this, in a nutshell, is the overriding message of the moral spectrum model. The more willing we are to expand our perspective on things, the more able we will be to make the best choices possible. Painting with just one color will hardly allow us to capture the world at all. With a handful of colors we do far better. And with the richest palette possible, our choices have the greatest likelihood of reflecting the infinite hues the universe we live in presents to us.

Can We Really Get Better?

Some people will say that all this talk about self-improvement in matters of morality sounds suspicious. It's too much like discussions about losing weight through dieting. Perhaps we *can* take incremental steps toward being better people, but it's only a matter of time before we'll fall back into our bad old ways. Like the dieter

---

[27]Bilimoria, Pursottama, "Indian Ethics," in Singer, Peter (Ed.), *A Companion to Ethics* (London: Blackwell, 1991), p. 52.

who can't help bingeing when he finds himself across the table from freshly-baked cheesecake, we, too, will be unable to restrain ourselves when we have the chance to commit adultery or fudge on our expense reports or claim a few additional deductions on our income tax.

This strikes me as a perfectly reasonable and quite realistic objection, but it's one that turns on a particular understanding of the word "diet." In this context, "diet" refers to all the things a person *isn't* going to eat. Think about it. When most of us say "I'm on a diet," we're letting others know that we are refraining from certain foods. "No cake for me," I say, "I'm dieting." Diet books tell us how to get by without carbohydrates or sugar or other favorite foods. Diet doctors give us programs for what foods we should steer clear of. The word "diet" has thus become synonymous with self-denial; it's all about restraining ourselves from what we really desire but won't allow ourselves to have.

There's another meaning of "diet," however. And here, by contrast, "diet" refers to what we *do* eat. To say, "I'm on a diet" is essentially redundant. We're *always* on a diet. My diet is the sum of choices I make about what *to* eat. Of course, I do choose not to eat certain things, but that's not where the focus is. Rather, when I talk about my diet, I'm talking about the foods that I will eat. My diet isn't about self-denial, it's about choice.

Morality can be looked at in the same way. Most of the time, the focus of ethics is on what's wrong. Morality tells us what we ought not to do. But it doesn't have to be this way. A richer appreciation of ethics understands it as providing guidance for how we *should* act. Morality isn't what restrains us; it's what leads us. Our systems of ethics don't steer us away from what's wrong; they point us toward what's right. We're not dieting when we choose to do the right thing; rather, our moral choices represent our steady diet of attitudes and behaviors that are most conducive to our long-term health.

Seen in this light, improving our ability to choose the right thing to do seems perfectly plausible. It's like any ongoing activity of self-improvement, from running to weightlifting to writing to painting. The more you do it, the better you get at it. And the better you get at it, the more you do.

It's Never Too Late to Be a Good Kid

Most of our beliefs about right and wrong were formed when we were kids. So it's perfectly natural that we should be far more focused on what's wrong than on what's right. The way we learned how to behave was mostly a matter of learning how *not* to behave. Ask parents how many times a day they tell their kids not to do something as compared to how many times they tell them to do something. If my own experience with my daughter is any gauge, the ratio is probably around twenty to one. And this is a shame, because it means that we tend to grow up being much more aware of what we shouldn't do than of what we should do. Even worse, we may come to believe that we constantly have to be told—and tell ourselves—what not to do. We may come to believe that we're basically bad people who have to be reined in by morality. We're naughty kids who need to be told "no" as often as possible.

But this is a mistake. There's no reason we have to keep replaying those old tapes. Just because we weren't perfect children doesn't mean that we're condemned to being that way for the rest of our lives. *It's never too late to be a good kid.* We can, even as adults, come to embrace our choice to do the right thing. We don't have to always feel as if we would prefer to do something we shouldn't. We don't have to always feel that it's only the threat of punishment—whether from our parents, the law, or God—that keeps us from being bad.

Science-fiction writer Isaac Asimov wondered about it this way: "Is the only reason you are virtuous because that's your ticket to heaven? Is the only reason you don't beat your children to death because you don't want to go to hell? It seems to me that it's insulting to human beings to imply that only a system of rewards and punishments can keep you a decent human being. Isn't it conceivable that a person wants to be a decent human being because that way he feels better? Because that way the world is better?"

Even as kids, we know that it feels better to be decent persons. Unfortunately, we often don't allow ourselves that sense of decency. We're usually too busy beating ourselves up for doing what we ought not to have done that we can't find a way to appreciate ourselves for doing what we should have.

When I was about seven, I had an elaborate ritual to help me find the decent person inside me. It was my way of repudiating the image I had of myself as a naughty little boy and getting closer to the sense that I really was a pretty good kid. Admittedly, it often had the effect of pleasing my parents, but that isn't why I did it. It was a matter of how I felt about myself, about the sort of person I saw myself as being.

When I am being punished—sent to my room to cool off—I lie down in the center of the circular rug next to my bunkbed. I stretch my arms out to its edges and stare at the ceiling. I close my eyes and pretend that I am rising up, hovering over the ground on a magic carpet. A honey-colored light emanates from above, bathing me in its golden glow. Warm vibrations pour over me, melting away my anger, frustration, nastiness—all the bad feelings inside me.

I feel the rug begin to spin: slowly at first, but then faster and faster until the outlines of the world blend together into a shimmering star. Then, like Superman exiting a phone booth Clark Kent has entered, I burst forth off of the rug a brand new person.

Then I stand, brush myself off, and go into my parents' room.

I sit down at my mother's dressing table and carefully dust off and arrange all her perfume and make-up bottles. I comb out all the hair in her hairbrush and throw it away. I wipe off the mirror with some Kleenex and make sure that all the tops on her powders and creams are screwed on securely. Then I push her dressing table chair squarely into its space and run a last hand over the back of it to catch any remaining dust particles.

Next, I go into my father's closet and get down on the floor under his hanging suits. A jumbled mass of shoes and shoe trees await me. First, I collect all the shoe trees. Usually, one or more is missing, so I have to dig around among loafers, wingtips, and winter boots to find them. When I've done so, I fit each shoe tree into its respective shoe and snug it in tight. Then I carefully pair up the shoes and arrange them side-by-side according to color and style. Dress shoes go to the far left with fanciness decreasing as you move right. When I place Dad's beat-up canvas lawnmowing shoes next to each other at the far right end of his closet, I am done.

I then go into the bathroom, comb my hair, brush my teeth, and wash my hands. If it's evening—and it usually is—I put my pajamas on and drop my dirty clothes down the laundry chute.

Finally, I tiptoe downstairs to where my parents are, either in the dining room finishing dinner, or in the living room, reading and listening to the stereo. Getting their attention, I announce in a clear unwavering voice: "Mom, Dad...the good little David has returned."

They both look up, smile knowingly, and return to whatever they are doing. I don't mind that they don't acknowledge my return with any great fanfare. It is enough for *me* to know that the good little David is back. Perhaps he won't stay long, but at least I know that he exists. I know that somewhere inside of me is a good person. I know I can be that person when I want to be, when I remember who he is. And that makes me feel good all over.

I think it's still the same today. The hard part, though, is remembering who that good little boy or girl is. Recognition can be fleeting; it's easy to forget that you're not an awful person . . . especially if you're wracked with guilt or shame over having done something regrettable.

One way to stay in touch with the good little boy or girl within you is to see beyond the boundaries of your current situation. Keep in mind that the choices we make don't define us instantly; added together, they define our character. One false step doesn't make you a bad person. Nor does one act of generosity make you wonderful.

Our choices are part of an ongoing legacy we are creating for ourselves and our communities. It is a moral legacy that we leave behind as a result of all that we have done and said. Examining this moral legacy—even as we are making it—allows us to put things in perspective and respond to our choices with greater wisdom. Ultimately, our moral legacy is who we really were; by reflecting upon it, we come to a better understanding of who we really are.

Chapter 7

Doing the Best We Can Do

Reflections on Our Moral Legacy

The Wrongness of Rightness

History's greatest horrors have been committed in the name of morality. Wars have been waged, pogroms enacted, injustices of every sort justified on the grounds of moral imperative. Might has traditionally made right, and those with the might have often considered it their right to do anything at all to ensure that their perception of rightness prevails.

The danger of intolerance grows as we become more assured that our viewpoint is the one true answer. When we're still figuring out where we stand on an issue we tend to be more open-minded. We're willing to accommodate differing perspectives in an effort to develop our own. We're less likely to close our minds to diverse viewpoints, especially if they can shed light on issues we're trying to make sense of ourselves.

Think of your own life. Remember when, as a teenager or young adult, you were beginning to form your own moral positions. Think of how willing you were to question everything, to challenge the beliefs you were brought up with, and to entertain even the most radical points of view. But that changed as soon as you settled on a position; then the intractability set in. You knew you were right and nothing was going to convince you otherwise. No longer did you listen to what others had to say to learn from them; you only listened so you could slam their point of view at every opportunity.

Most of us tend to dig in and hold on to our moral positions for a couple of reasons. First, because we're afraid: our moral views play a major role in who we are. We define ourselves in no small part by what we think is right and wrong. To call those beliefs into question is tantamount to calling our identity into question. So we're reluctant to challenge our moral beliefs for fear of undermining our sense of self. This is perfectly understandable, but it doesn't always represent the most reasonable way to be.

Imagine, for example, that you've always seen yourself as someone who is adamantly in favor of personal liberty when it comes to the wearing of motorcycle helmets. You've always considered yourself something of the swashbuckling type, and that runs counter to the idea that society might have a compelling reason to insist that cyclists protect themselves from themselves. Suppose, though, there comes a time in your life when—having examined the issue from new perspectives—you find yourself sympathizing with the view that helmet laws actually do have merit. Chances are you will resist this conclusion—even if it is the right one. You know yourself, as do your close friends and family, as someone opposed to such laws. So it's not going to be easy or automatic to suddenly change. In fact, you may even dig in deeper to your original position, even to the point of ignoring the very evidence that persuaded you to consider changing.

A second reason that we become intolerant is because we *adopt*—as opposed to *formulate*—our moral views. Instead of gathering information and developing our own judgment of what's right and wrong, we simply take someone else's word for it. We say "ditto" to the judgment of our friends, religious leaders, or favorite talk-show hosts without really having arrived at that judgment ourselves. This isn't to say that their position is necessarily a bad one; it may indeed be one that we would arrive at independently if we considered the issue ourselves. What's problematic is the unreflective acceptance of the view. Because when we adopt someone else's judgment without engaging in the process that led to that judgment, we're less likely to have good reasons for our position. And without good reasons, we're less likely to be tolerant of others' points of view. We're more likely to dig in to where we stand and close our minds to divergent perspectives.

Finally, a third and perhaps most common reason for our intolerance is that we fail to see the big picture. We forget that our moral positions transcend our own experience, that they significantly affect the lives of those around us and those who follow us.

In short, we forget to take into account our *moral legacy*. We either fail or refuse to see that our lives are bigger than our lives, that the choices we make have wide-ranging implications, and that our moral legacy will remain long after we are gone.

Ironically, however, there's no escaping it. Every choice we make goes into creating our moral legacy. None of us gets a special "get out of jail free" card when it comes to how we will be remembered. Of course, it's perfectly possible to hide the truth or to cover up embarrassing or shameful facts about ourselves. But that doesn't change the embarrassing or shameful fact of the matter . . . whether or not we admit it to anyone else—or even ourselves.

So it behooves us to live our lives in a way that distinguishes our moral legacy. To do so is to live such that we are crafting a coherent narrative of our days, a story in which the character we are playing reflects our true character, in which the choices we make represent an authentic expression of our deepest values, in which our moral legacy really reflects how we would most like to be remembered.

The principles that we've explored here have been intended to help us to do just that: to increase the likelihood that the choices we make are consistent with the person we want to be and would like to have been. These various ways of approaching moral issues have been meant to expand our moral palettes so we can broaden our perspectives and make more sophisticated choices about the right thing to do. While the principles can be used independently of one another, they also fit together as a kind of algorithm for deciding how we should act. We might employ it as follows:

Step 1: Ask the Seven Moral Prism questions:

E Existentialist prism:

"What course(s) of action will set people most free?"

D Deontological prism:

"What would I do if everyone in the world were to do as I did?"

C Ethic of Caring prism:

"What course(s) of action will best sustain and nurture a caring relationship between myself and others?"

C Communitarian prism:

"How would I act if everyone in my community knew exactly what I was doing?"

U Utilitarian prism:

"What course(s) of action will best maximize total happiness in the world?"

V Virtue Ethics prism:

"What would the most virtuous person I know of do in this situation?"

E Egoist prism:

"What course(s) of action will most effectively ensure that my short- and long-term goals are reached?"

Do these seven perspectives yield a consistent answer as to what you ought to do? If you are fully confident that the answer is yes, go for it. If not, proceed to Step 2.

Step 2: Ask which course of action would represent the best alignment between your virtues and your values. What choice would best express what you care about in a way that is consistent with who you want to be?

Does this give you a clear answer as to what you ought to do? If so, go ahead and do it. If not, proceed to Step 3.

Step 3: Ask which course of action would best express the Golden Rule.

Does this provide a definitive answer as to what you ought to do? If so, go ahead and do it. If not, proceed to Step 4.

Step 4: Consider nature as your oracle. How do you interpret what nature is telling you ought to be done? What course of action best represents a loving touch? What course of action is in nature's best interest?

Does this answer the question of what you ought to do? If so, do it. If not, proceed to Step 5.

Step 5: What course of action will make you more likely to do the right thing in the future? What choice will increase your appetite for doing the right thing?

Does this give you a clear idea of the direction to take? If so, take it. If not, proceed to Step 6.

Step 6: What is the best you can do? What course of action represents your best shot at doing the right thing?

Having gone through steps 1–5 without a definitive answer, what choice can you live with? Which choice, if it turns out to be wrong, offers you the best chance for making changes in the future?

More often than not, the right thing to do will emerge as we work through the steps. But it is possible—and not entirely uncommon—that we will arrive at Step 6 without a clear directive for acting. At this point, therefore, the best that we can do is the best that we can do. Nobody's perfect, and our moral legacy won't be either. So we need to be willing to recognize that occasionally—and perhaps more often than that—we will make mistakes. And we need to be willing to make them and learn from them and do better next time. We need to be willing to do the best we can do, even if it's not all that great.

When Doing the Best We Can Do Is the Best We Can Do

After I wrote and thought about the chapter that opened this book, I decided that I ought to talk to my father about it. After all, he featured prominently in the story and probably had recollections of that day in Montana that I had forgotten. More important, I felt quite strongly that we had a moral duty to discuss it. Our shared silence regarding the incident represented, I thought, a moral failing on our part. Were we to consider our lack of dialogue in light of our moral legacy, we would have to realize that words needed to be spoken. We couldn't go on pretending it hadn't happened or that we had dealt with it appropriately.

So I printed out a copy of the section entitled *A Gas Station Burns in the Forest: Illuminating Our Moral Legacy* and mailed it to him. A week passed. Ten days. A fortnight. This was surprising. My father and I had a fairly vital correspondence; we usually traded a couple of letters a month. It was especially odd not to hear back when I had specifically asked for his feedback. My father was quite outspoken; it would be highly unusual for him to pass up an opportunity to tell me what he thought. I began to fear that I might have hurt his feelings or angered him in recounting the story. I began to wonder if I had done the right thing in sending it to him.

I was going to call him on Sunday—as I often did—and ask him if he felt I was out of line. I was going to inquire whether he would prefer that I not include the story in this book or if he thought I should change the names of the people involved to protect his identity.

But on Saturday I got a call from home. Unexpectedly, it was my mom—who rarely phones, especially in the middle of the day.

She says to me the words that as an adult child, I have half-expected and fully-feared with every long-distance phone call: "Come home quickly, your father is dying."

I feel the ground come up and slam me in the face. A gray cylinder slides down over my body blocking out everything in the world but the phone receiver in my hand.

My mom explains that my father's kidneys, which haven't been in the best of shape for some years now, have begun to fail. His doctor gives him less than two weeks to live.

Staggered, I get as much information as I can and make plans to fly in as soon as possible.

With these details out of the way, my mom and I transition somewhat clumsily into a semi-normal conversation. I ask her if Dad got my recent letter. She said it arrived, but that he was too out of it to read it.

And so, I think, I have failed. I have waited too long to talk with my father about that day in Montana. And now, it will never be. The sand has slid through the hourglass, gone forever.

That's when my mom says she's read what I've sent. And she tells me that she and my father have talked about the incident on several occasions. "Your father could never forget that," she says, "and he always wondered if he'd done the right thing. He was scared, you know. And he wanted to get you and Timmy to safety. After he told the park rangers what had happened, he thought about going back to help. But he thought his first responsibility was to you boys. If something had happened to him, he didn't know who would take care of you."

I mumble a few words about wishing I had sent him the story sooner; if only we could have talked about it.

Mom concurs. "I think he would have liked to talk about it with you, too. I know he felt that he ought perhaps to have behaved differently—or maybe done something more. I think he would have appreciated the opportunity to explain what was going on for him at the time."

I choke back a sob and apologize for failing to do what I should have done much sooner. Why didn't I send the letter a month ago? Years ago? Why was I such a coward? How can I ever forgive myself?

My mother consoles me. "David, you did the best you could. Your father knows that. Just as you know he did the best he could, as well. And he knows you know that about him, too. You can't spend the rest of your life torturing yourself about what didn't happen. You did the best you could do and that's all you could do."

She's right, of course. What's done—or not done—is done. I can't change the past. And I couldn't even at the time; I was, as my mom pointed out, doing the best that I could do with the information and abilities I had. That in retrospect I can see that I would have done better had I behaved differently is beside the point. There will always be room to choose more wisely—no matter what choices we make. The best we can do, however, is to make the best choices we can at the time: to be as thoughtful and compassionate as we know how to be, knowing full well that it will always be possible to be far more thoughtful and compassionate than we ever are.

We can also resolve to keep striving to be better, to keep learning from our past mistakes, and to behave differently, with more wisdom, next time. In my case, this means being willing to face the deep questions that arose for my father and me on that day in Montana. It means having the courage to wonder aloud whether we did the right thing and to draw upon the difficult lessons of what happened to do better in the future.

So, I have talked about it with my mom and my sister. I got in touch with my old friend who was with my father and me on that trip and discussed it with him, too. In recalling the incident for this book, I've had the opportunity to talk about it with my wife and friends and colleagues who have seen drafts of the manuscript. It hasn't always been easy, but I think it's been the right thing to do. And I feel that I am honoring my father's memory each time I remember what happened and use it as a way to think about how to do better from here on out.

I did the best I could do with him in the past; I owe it to him—and to the world he has left—to do the best I can do now and in the future.

Hearing Our Own Eulogy:
The Legacy of Our Moral Legacy

In Mark Twain's *The Adventures of Tom Sawyer,* Tom, Huck Finn, and Joe Harper enjoy an opportunity that none of us can reasonably look forward to: they get to attend their own funeral and hear the sermon preached in their remembrance. Twain describes what the boys, who are believed by their townspeople to have drowned in the Mississippi river, witness from their hiding place in the unused church gallery:

> As the service proceeded, the clergyman drew such pictures of the graces, the winning ways, and the rare promise of the lost lads that every soul there, thinking he recognized these pictures, felt a pang in remembering that he had persistently blinded himself to them always before, and had as persistently seen only faults and flaws in the poor boys. The minister related many a touching incident in the lives of the departed, too, which illustrated their sweet, generous natures, and the people could easily see, now, how noble and beautiful those episodes were, and remembered with grief that at the time they occurred they had seemed rank rascalities, well deserving of the cowhide. The congregation became more and more moved, as the pathetic tale

went on, till at last the whole company broke down and joined the weeping mourners in a chorus of anguished sobs, the preacher himself giving way to his feelings, and crying in the pulpit. [28]

Who wouldn't give anything to have that same opportunity? Who wouldn't love to experience such an outpouring of affection from friends, family members, and townspeople? Wouldn't most of us, like Tom, seriously consider faking our own demise in order to find out just how we were being remembered?

Our legacy naturally intrigues us. It's perfectly understandable that we would want to know how the world will recall us after we're gone. The question is: How many of us will be surprised? How many of us are living our lives so that our legacy will reflect all that we truly hold most near and dear? How many of us, in other words, are living our lives with integrity, where integrity is defined as being the same person you are when you're alone as you are when you're not?

Reflecting on our moral legacy, and in light of it, doing the best that we can offers real hope for achieving that sort of integrity in our lives. Expanding our moral palette and making choices accordingly provides us with a means to ensure that the person we are and the person we will have been are one and the same. Thus, by distinguishing our moral legacy through our choices and behaviors, we are able to share in that unique experience Tom Sawyer and his friends enjoyed: we give ourselves the opportunity to hear how we will be remembered—for we live our lives in such a manner that our moral legacy and our moral lives are one.

May we all have the wisdom to perceive and choose the right thing to do, and in doing so, leave a moral legacy that distinguishes our lives, our memories, and ourselves.

---

[28]Twain, Mark, *The Adventures of Tom Sawyer* (Oxford Text Archive), p. 176.

Suggestions for Further Reading

For readers interested in exploring philosophical ethics in greater depth, I would suggest that you consider taking an introductory ethics course at your local university or community college. It tends to be easier and more fruitful to study these issues under the guidance of a teacher and in conjunction with fellow students. With that in mind though, I offer the following somewhat eclectic list of readings as a starting point for further investigation into ethics and morality. Most are books I consulted in one way or another during the writing of *Choosing the Right Thing to Do;* nearly all of them have useful bibliographies that can lead the interested reader deeper into the field.

Anderson, Elizabeth, *Value in Ethics and Economics* (Cambridge: Harvard University Press, 1993).

Aristotle, *Nicomachean Ethics* (available in many translations, W. D. Ross' is highly recommended).

Baier, Annette, *Moral Prejudices: Essays on Ethics* (Cambridge: Harvard University Press, 1994).

Beauchamp, Tom L., and Bowie, Norman E., (Eds.), *Ethical Theory and Business* (New Jersey: Prentice-Hall, 1997).

Berry, Wendell, *The Gift of the Good Land* (San Francisco: North Point, 1981).

Blackburn, Simon, *Essays in Quasi-Realism* (New York: Oxford University Press, 1993).

Brandt, Richard B., *A Theory of the Good and the Right* (Oxford: Clarendon Press, 1979).

Broad, C. D., *Five Types of Ethical Theory* (New York: Harcourt, Brace, 1930).

Coles, Robert, *The Moral Life of Children* (Boston: Atlantic Monthly Press, 1986).

Dawkins, Richard, *The Selfish Gene* (Oxford: Oxford University Press, 1989).

Dewey, John, *Ethics* (New York: Henry Holt, 1932).

Gibbard, Allan, *Wise Choices, Apt Feelings: A Theory of Normative Judgment* (Cambridge: Harvard University Press, 1990).

Gilligan, Carol, *In a Different Voice: Psychological Theory and Women's Development* (Cambridge: Harvard University Press, 1982).

Hare, R.M., *Moral Thinking* (Oxford: Oxford University Press, 1981).

Hume, David, *A Treatise of Human Nature*, L.A. Selby-Bigge/Nidditch edition (Oxford: Oxford University Press, 1989).

Kant, Immanuel, *Groundwork of the Metaphysics of Morals* (1785) [trans. Paton] (London: Hutchinson, 1948).

Kohlberg, Lawrence, *Essays in Moral Development,* Vol. I, *The Philosophy of Moral Development: Moral Stages and the Idea of Justice* (New York: Harper & Row, 1981).

Leider, Richard J., and Shapiro, David, *Repacking Your Bags: Lighten Your Load for the Rest of Your Life* (San Francisco: Berrett-Koehler, 1995).

Locke, John, *An Essay Concerning Human Understanding* (vol. 1) (London: Dent & Sons, 1961).

MacIntyre, Alisdair, *A Short History of Ethics* (New York: Macmillan, 1966).

MacIntyre, Alisdair, *After Virtue: A Study in Moral Theory* (Notre Dame: Notre Dame Press, 1984).

Mackie, J. L., *Ethics: Inventing Right and Wrong* (Harmondsworth: Penguin, 1977).

McNaughton, David, *Moral Vision: An Introduction to Ethics* (NY: Blackwell, 1988).

Mill, John Stuart, *Utilitarianism*, (1863).

Moore, G. E., *Principia Ethica* (Cambridge: Cambridge University Press, 1993).

Murdoch, Iris, *The Sovereignty of the Good* (London: Routledge & Kegan Paul, 1970).

Needleman, Jacob, *The Heart of Philosophy* (San Francisco: Harper, 1982).

Noddings, Nel, *Caring: A Feminine Approach to Ethics and Education* (Berkeley: University of California Press, 1978).

Persig, Robert, *Zen and the Art of Motorcycle Maintenance* (New York: Bantam, 1974).

Plato, *Euthyphro* [trans. Tredennick] in *The Last Days of Socrates* (Harmondsworth: Penguin Book, 1969).

Plato, *Republic* [trans. Grube] (Indianapolis: Hackett, 1974).

Quinn, Daniel, *Ishmael* (New York: Bantam/Turner, 1992).

Rawls, John, *A Theory of Justice* (Oxford: Oxford University Press, 1971).

Ross, W. D., *The Right and the Good* (Oxford: Clarendon Press, 1930).

Sartre, Jean-Paul, *Existentialism is a Humanism* (1946) [trans. P. Mairet] (London: Methuen, 1950).

Sayre-McCord, Geoffrey (Ed.), *Essays in Moral Realism* (Ithaca: Cornell University Press, 1988).

Singer, Peter (Ed.), *A Companion to Ethics* (London: Blackwell, 1993).

Smith, Adam, *The Theory of Moral Sentiments* (New York: Augustus M. Kelley, 1966).

Spinoza, Benedict de, *The Ethics,* in *A Spinoza Reader* {Trans. Curley, Edwin} (Princeton: Princeton University Press, 1994).

Thompson, Paul (Ed.), *Issues in Evolutionary Ethics* (Albany: SUNY Press, 1995).

Thoreau, Henry David, *Walden* (many editions).

Wilson, E. O., *Sociobiology: The New Synthesis* (Cambridge: Harvard University Press, 1975).

Wilson, James Q., *The Moral Sense* (New York: Macmillan, 1993).

Index

caring, ethic of, 43, 45, 47, 49, 51,
59–61, 74
examples of approach, 73, 79,
123
categorical imperative, 44–45, 57,
118–119
character, 2
charity, 70
Chekhov, Anton, 110
children
and friendships, 110–112,
127–130
as judges of integrity, 197–199
parent-child relationship,
130–137
choices. *See* moral choices
client/customer relationships, 114,
141–144
See also stakeholder theory
colleagues, relationships with, 114
See also business ethics
Collier, John, 155–156
communitarianism, 43, 45–46, 47,
49, 51, 61–63, 73–74
examples of communitarian view,
79, 123
See also Hume, David
compassion, 60
conflicts of interest, 95–98
consequences (outcomes), as moral
guide, 42, 47, 58, 68, 72–73,
124
"continent" people, 181
corporate responsibility, stakeholder
theory of, 139–141
See also business ethics
courage, 6, 93
customer/client relationships, 114,
141–144
See also stakeholder theory

Dawkins, Richard, 154, 155
deontology, 21–22, 43, 44–45, 47,
49–50, 51, 55–58
examples of deontological view,
73, 79, 123, 152, 159
See also Kant, Immanuel
descriptive properties, vs. normative
properties, 171
desires, indulgence/satisfaction of,
105–107, 180–182
Dewey, John, 16

diet, two meanings of, 201
Dixon, Bob, 85–86, 87, 89–91
Dixon, Jennifer, 68–69, 190–191
Drucker, Peter, 140
duty, in deontological theory,
21–22, 44, 58

egoism, 43, 46–47, 49, 51, 68–71, 74
examples of egoist view, 73, 79,
123
See also self-interest
Emerson, Ralph Waldo, 148
emotions
evolutionary views of, 88–89,
155, 191–192
feelings-principles spectrum, 42,
43, 71–72
as moral guide, 42, 72
vs. reason, as source of motivation, 21–22, 170
environmental disputes, approaches
for resolving, 159–160, 167
Environmental Protection Agency
(EPA), 86, 87
ethical leadership, 83
ethical relativism, 23, 24–26, 33, 60
ethic of caring, 43, 45, 47, 49, 51,
55, 59–61, 74
examples of approach, 73, 79,
123
Euthyphro (Plato), 21
evolutionary views of emotions,
88–89, 155, 191–192
evolutionary views of moral behavior, 88–89, 147–148, 151,
154–157
existentialism, 39, 40, 43–44, 49,
51, 52–55, 73–74
examples of existentialist view,
73, 79, 123

facts, and implication of moral responsibility, 170–173
fear, 6
feelings. *See* emotions
feelings-principles spectrum, 42, 43,
71–72
forgetfulness, 8
Frank, Robert, 88, 155
freedom, maximization of, in existentialist theory, 44, 49, 54–55
Freeman, Edward, 139

About the Author

David A. Shapiro is a writer, consultant, and curriculum designer specializing in progressive business and personal development programs. He is also Education Director for the Northwest Center Philosophy for Children, a non-profit organization that brings philosophy into the lives of young people in schools and community groups through literature, philosophical works, and classroom activities.

David began his professional writing career by penning jokes for stand-up comedians but eventually realized it would be much funnier to write corporate training materials. As an employee of several internationally-known training organizations, he spent more than a decade writing and designing numerous interactive multimedia programs intended to help businesspeople maximize their personal and professional effectiveness.

Branching out on his own, he began to explore how people's basic philosophical viewpoints contributed to their levels of success and fulfillment at home and on the job. In support of this, he completed a BA in Philosophy at the University of Minnesota and an MA in Philosophy at the University of Washington, where he is currently in the process of finishing up his Ph.D.

David is co-author of *Repacking Your Bags: Lighten Your Load for the Rest of Your Life* with Richard J. Leider, which has sold more than 200,000 copies in the U.S. and Japan. He considers the choice to repack his bags and return to graduate school a pretty good example of walking his repacking talk.

David lives in Seattle with his wife Jennifer Dixon and their daughter Amelia Dixon-Shapiro.